M000119238

ADVANCE PRAISE

(Contributors Listed in Alphabetical Order)

"Brig Gen (USA, Ret) Peter Zwack—a treasured friend and professional colleague—has published a remarkable portrayal of his 2008–2009 tour in Afghanistan. His first-hand insights into a complex nation—its history, geography, culture, and sociology—provide an essential treatise for experts and laymen alike. Written in a uniquely personal diary style, *Afghanistan Kabul Kurier* is an invaluable primer for anyone who wants to understand the tumultuous events of today."

—Lieutenant General James R. Clapper Jr. (Ret) U.S. Air Force
Former Director of National Intelligence (DNI), 2010–2017
Undersecretary of Defense for Intelligence, 2007–2010
Author of: *Facts and Fears, Hard Truths from a Life in Intelligence*

"In a sharp-focused and unsentimental portrait of a place and a people we never truly understood, Peter Zwack details the year he spent heading military intelligence in Afghanistan. His overriding message is a somber one: "Trying to fix what was already broken beyond repair will never work."

—Robert Cowley
Founding Editor, The Quarterly Journal of Military History
Author of: *What If?: The World's Foremost Military Historians Imagine What Might Have Been*

"An insightful, informative, and delightful read of a critical time in our two-decade-long experience in Afghanistan. In light of recent events and a tumultuous withdrawal, Peter Zwack's testimonial of an inflection point in our Afghan mission reminds us that counter-insurgency efforts in this war-torn country were neither futile nor their eventual outcome a forgone conclusion. Peter's tale is one of deep respect for history, culture, and ingrained realities. Peter is pragmatic, clear-eyed in assessing the internal context and challenges, and provides a justified glimmer of hope had we pursued limited aims with the perseverance, strategic patience, and minimum resources they called for."

—Major General Gordon "Skip" Davis Jr, U.S. Army (Ret)
Director of Operations, J3, U.S. European Command, 2016–2018
Commander, CSTC-A, Afghanistan, 2015–2016, Senior ISAF Staff, 2008–2009
Deputy Chief of Staff for Operations and Intel, NATO, 2013–2015

"It was an honor and a pleasure for me to know Peter Zwack in Afghanistan, and I am sure that the readers of this book will find the same pleasure as they discover Afghanistan through his experience. Unlike many in military or diplomatic leadership, Peter was committed to knowing Afghanistan personally, with openness and honesty—and without trepidation. My best memories of Peter were "outside the wire," where he could really experience Afghanistan in all its beauty, complexity, and confounding contradiction. How lucky we are that he is sharing those experiences now. Although many will enter the ongoing debate over Afghanistan through books and essays, few will be able to rely on such direct and very human engagement. No one will ever have to debate Peter's contributions. Every Afghan he met will have been touched by the best that America had to offer."

—David Gallalee
United Nations (UNAMA), Department of State, and NATO
Afghanistan, 2007–2015

"A phenomenal and personal tale—one that most Americans don't get to see—of a deployed senior intelligence officer and his role in analysis and decision-making. Having worked closely with Peter Zwack in peacetime and combat, this excellent memoir addresses the extreme challenges, unique complexities, myriad cultures, and puzzling dynamics faced by U.S. and NATO forces in Afghanistan. What makes this book particularly fascinating is Peter's masterful approach to telling the story … he shares the information, but he also bares his soul. A gripping read."

—Mark Hertling, Lieutenant General (Ret), U.S. Army
Commander US Army Europe, 2011–2012
Commander of Multi-National Division North, Iraq, 2007–2009
Author of: _Growing Physician Leaders_

"Peter Zwack combines on-the-ground military experience with an unparalleled grasp of Afghanistan's brutal history; uncanny powers of observation; physical courage; and the restless spirit of a 19th-century adventurer. Those of us who were privileged to read his private dispatches from Kabul during his service as our top military intelligence officer on the ground got an honest, unadorned view of the reality of a harsh land gripped, yet again, by war. At a time when bureaucrats and journalists alike pushed self-interested agendas, Peter sought to understand adversaries and allies on their own revealing terms. Known to insiders as a brilliant "intel hand," he waged war bravely, thought clearly, wrote enthrallingly, and spoke truthfully. Anyone who wants to reach beyond the misleading cliches about Afghanistan should start with this remarkable eyewitness book."

—Ralph Peters
Author of: _Cain at Gettysburg_ and _Beyond Terror_

"B.G. (r) Peter Zwack's very personal *Afghanistan Kabul Kurier* is about as authentic a first-hand account of senior-level soldiering in Afghanistan as I've seen. As the former NATO Commander from 2009–2013, Afghanistan was every day on my scope. By knitting together the issues of a decade ago and the very real challenges facing our nation and allies today, Peter's powerful and highly insightful read supplies valuable context for what is unfolding in Afghanistan. Of special note, this unique memoir is as much about the complex people and cultural geography in and around that ancient nation as it is about military operations—which makes Peter's journal invaluable for practitioners, academia, and the general public alike."

—Admiral James G. Stavridis, Ph.D., U.S. Navy (Ret)
16th Supreme Allied Commander, NATO
Dean of the Fletcher School of International Relations at Tufts University,
2013–2018
Author of bestselling: *2034 A novel of the Next World War*

"Peter Zwack brings the reader into the moments inside the U.S. intelligence center in Afghanistan. What was told to us? What did Peter and his staff believe? How transient was truth compared to what our intelligence analysts believed then? Peter Zwack provides a perspective and a lens into what the intelligence community once believed and why they believed it back then."

—Bing West
Author of bestsellers: *The Wrong War* and *The Last Platoon*

AFGHANISTAN
KABUL KURIER

April 12th, 2022

Honored Nate to

AFGHANISTAN
KABUL KURIER

Years of Your Stellar

One Soldier's Story
of the Taliban,
Tribes & Loyalties,
Opium Trade,
& Burqas

Service by your very
Proud Father-in-law...

BRIGADIER GENERAL PETER B. ZWACK (RET)

Semper Fi from an
Friendly Army Friend!

Afghanistan Kabul Kurier

Brigadier General Peter B. Zwack (Ret)
U.S. Defense Attaché to the Russian Federation 2012–2014.
Wilson Center Global Fellow, The Kennan Institute

Deployed to Afghanistan 2008–2009
Director of the Joint Intelligence Operations Center

First Edition

ISBN: 978-1-7340060-3-2 (Paperback)
ISBN: 978-1-7340060-4-9 (Hardcover)
ISBN: 978-1-7340060-7-0 (Large Print)
ISBN: 978-1-7340060-6-3 (ePub)
ISBN: 978-1-7340060-5-6 (Audio Book)

Library of Congress Control Number: 2021919985

Zwack Eurasia Consultancy LLC

All photos are courtesy of the author unless otherwise indicated.

https://peterbzwack.net

DEDICATION

TO THE DEPLOYED MILITARY AND civilians, American and international, who served selflessly and bravely to defend our nations and strove to help Afghanistan become a safer, more inclusive nation. God bless the memory of those souls who lost their lives or were maimed in this noble endeavor. Most of all now, God bless their bereaved families and loved ones.

Special thanks to the great men and women of our JIOC-A team, who worked so hard on this mission and loyally supported me while always maintaining their balance and humor in this difficult and stressful environment.

Deep appreciation to my family – my wife Stephanie, and my children, Broghan, Peter Jr and Alessandra – who supported me throughout, and to those countless thousands of family members for their own sacrifices supporting those deployed in this long and difficult endeavor.

Heartfelt wishes to the long-suffering but proudly resilient Afghan people from all walks of life who deserve a safer, more representative future. You will not be forgotten.

AFGHANISTAN

TABLE OF CONTENTS

General David D. McKiernan

FOREWORD

I WAS ONCE TOLD THAT history should not be written until at least fifty years after an event so that all the proper research, analysis, and perspective are incorporated. Of course, that won't stop all the "experts" from opining on the tragedy of Afghanistan and its people. There will undoubtedly be a plethora of books, articles, essays, and so on written about that country over the next couple of years that will be incomplete or even misleading.

This book is a notable exception. Peter Zwack has provided in his *Afghanistan Kabul Kurier* diary a refreshing "in the moment" series of reflections on his year-long stay in Afghanistan in 2008 and 2009—offering perspective on the analysis and decisions that were being made at that time. Merging history, culture, demographics, topography, and a tactical-to-strategic military appreciation, Zwack's journal is a fascinating look at the country through the eyes of a senior intelligence officer as events are unfolding. It also captures BG Zwack's personal routine in an unfamiliar environment, far removed from family and previous assignments.

This first-hand account is a must-read for military leaders, foreign service officers, and the full range of interagency professionals who will likely serve someday in a place they knew little about before they arrived. In Peter's case, it was in a war zone, a coalition environment, in a land very unknown by most prior to 2001.

The *Afghanistan Kabul Kurier* tells a great story in a very readable, personalized style that reflects who Peter Zwack is—soldier, intelligence expert, man for all seasons, and an intellectual equipped with a keen sense of history and a people-oriented outlook. It was my honor to have him serve in the ISAF headquarters under my command, and he remains a close friend to this day.

—David D. McKiernan
General (Ret), U.S. Army
Commander ISAF/US forces Afghanistan, 2008-2009

INTRODUCTION

IF YOU HAVE PICKED UP this book, odds are good that you have also seen news footage and images of the massive airlift at Kabul International Airport in late August 2021. The spectacle of thousands of frightened people pleading to escape the incoming Taliban regime was—and will always be—heartbreaking. The suicide bomber attack at the airport on August 26 only added to the horror. During a long career in military intelligence, I've witnessed more than one tragedy first-hand. Still, the images of anguish and violence at and around the airport as the August 31 evacuation deadline approached are among the most gut-wrenching I've ever seen.

Those images of chaos, desperation, and death will stay with us for years to come (as they should.) But in truth, they represent only a brief (if exquisitely painful) moment in a long, long saga. The story of how we got to where we are in Afghanistan in 2021 begins long before U.S. military intervention in 2001 after 9/11...long before the Soviets tried and failed in their 1980s intervention...long before the British and Russians used Afghanistan in their geopolitical chess match—the so-called Great Game—in the 1800s.

How we—meaning the world community—reached such a low point in Afghanistan in 2021 stretches back not decades, not centuries, but millennia.

We in the modern West often have difficulty grasping the depth and breadth of cultural memory and tribal loyalties in places like Afghanistan. The country is quite literally the crossroads of Southwest Asia. The Silk Road—the storied 4,000-mile trade route that connected China with Europe and Africa two thousand years ago—crossed the heart of Afghanistan. The travelers and traders who moved up and down its length carried with them a magical mix of art, philosophy, aesthetics, beliefs, and traditions from dozens of civilizations—some of which Afghanistan absorbed and made its own. During the heyday of the "Hippie Trail" in the 1960s and 1970s, young nomads from the U.S. and elsewhere trekked through Afghanistan to explore the country's rich cultural landscape. Many no doubt saw what I did when I traveled to our units and headquarters around Afghanistan in 2008 and 2009—echoes of a grand and glorious antiquity. Even in a state of decay, the beauty and craftsmanship of architecture and art created centuries ago will take your breath away. No wonder, then, that average Afghans living among these splendid ruins measure Time in centuries, not years.

Unfortunately, the wealth and sophisticated cultures that flourished in cities and sites along the Silk Road attracted the unwanted attention of a long series of ambitious invaders, including Alexander the Great, the Persian Safavids, and legendarily lethal Mongols. Over the centuries, armies swept across Afghanistan, seizing people and land, often laying waste to entire cities. During these invasions, the people of Afghanistan were slaughtered, conquered, or driven to the safety of the massive and hard-to-penetrate Hindu-Kush Mountain range that dominates the region.

No surprise, these remote mountain and valley sanctuaries became permanent homes for generations of Afghans. Suspicion toward outsiders, low literacy rates, and bone-deep adherence to age-old traditions forged a proud and insular culture of independent warriors willing to fight to the death anyone and anything that threatened to disrupt their way of life. Even residents of neighboring valleys were (and still are) viewed with distaste and distrust. To a lesser degree, the mountain mindset also permeated the lowlands at the foot of the Hindu-Kush.

Fast forward to the late 1970s, when the latest chapter of Afghanistan's troubles with outsiders began in earnest. In 1979, the USSR launched a campaign to seize the country and prop up its failing communist government. Despite its long history of fiercely and proudly defending its own borders, Moscow miscalculated—ironically—the ferocious and sustained pushback from Afghans in the hinterlands who had no intention of giving up their homeland, then or ever. Exhausted and financially crippled by a decade of failed effort to subjugate the Afghans, the Soviets limped home across their border in 1989. Sadly, we all know what happened next: thirty years of internal upheaval, during which six million Afghans—a population equivalent to the entire state of Maryland or Missouri—were uprooted. During that three-decade period, the world witnessed the birth and growth of extremist movements in the region, the horror of the 9/11 attacks, and the beginning of a multi-national effort to eradicate the Taliban, al-Qaeda, ISIS, and their twisted take on ancient Islam.

That's where I come into the story. In June 2008, I was deployed as a senior Colonel to Afghanistan to assume the role of Director of the Joint Intelligence and Operations Center, or JIOC-A at NATO's International Security and Assistance Force (ISAF) Headquarters in Kabul. At that point, the international coalition effort had been underway roughly six years. The mission's first two years were filled with optimism about bringing international terrorists to heel, helping average Afghans reclaim some semblance of day-to-day security, and battling longstanding corruption to create a functioning and credible central government. One of the biggest concerns was the outsized role of poppy-growing and the opium trade in the country's agrarian-based economy.

Unfortunately, the fledgling Afghanistan effort took a hit in March 2003 when a second front in the so-called War on Terror was launched in Iraq. At that point, international resources—military, intelligence, economic, and more—were stretched thin between the two major efforts, with Iraq taking the lion's share. The operation in Kabul and elsewhere in Afghanistan was perceived by many to be understaffed, underfunded and (perhaps) underappreciated compared to its sister operation in Baghdad.

As you'll read in these pages, when I arrived in Kabul in June 2008, the challenges my team and I faced were plentiful. Our ISAF intelligence center was housed in the dark basement of an old building in a military compound that had seen far better days. Power could be intermittent; days were long; the work was non-stop. Camp security had been beefed up in the previous couple of years, thanks to a rise in insurgent attacks around Kabul. (Rockets sent us scrambling to our camp bunker in the middle of the night more than once.) The increase in attacks meant that ISAF soldiers and staff could no longer move about Kabul freely—getting to know locals and projecting a friendly presence. That said, we were well taken care of by an international staff.

For me, the enhanced security was both a blessing and a curse. I appreciated the vital need to protect the camp and everyone in it, but I had learned from my service and travels worldwide that even the best piped-in intelligence is no match for first-hand observation. (As a young U.S. Army officer studying Russian language and culture with an American college group in the Soviet provincial city of Tver in 1989, I discovered that bootlegged vodka and midnight ice hockey games were great ways to get to know the locals.) Gregarious by nature, I thrived on getting out and about to see things for myself, meet residents and absorb gobs of information about local business, customs, history, and—of course—politics. Only by getting behind and beyond the official picture of a place is it possible to build the context you need to understand what's truly going on.

As you'll see, I pushed to get "outside the gates" of our Kabul compound several times during my year-long deployment. Some of my forays out were in armored SUVs in which all passengers were dressed in nondescript clothes and (discreetly) armed with guns

… an M4 automatic rifle tucked away on the floorboard, for good measure. Other trips involved ear-splitting rides in huge military choppers up and over Afghanistan's utterly breathtaking mountains. (The highest peak in the country is magnificent Noshaq. At 24,500 feet, it soars more than four miles straight up into the sky.) In all cases, I drank in the scenery, from goat-herding families living in mud-walled farmsteads to the claustrophobia-inducing darkness of the incredible Salang Tunnel through the Hindu-Kush, to the haunting ruins of too many palaces and mosques to count.

My year conducting intel operations and analysis at Kabul felt at once endless and too short. One of the chief things that helped me maintain my equilibrium was keeping a diary of my experience. I tried to write a page every night before retiring for the day. During rare quiet moments, I sifted and compiled my thoughts on Friday mornings (the Islamic day of prayer) into a multi-page missive that I nicknamed the *Kabul Kurier*, which I would send off roughly quarterly to family, associates, and friends. ("Kurier" means courier or messenger in German—I had created its predecessor, the *Kosovo Kurier* when I served as chief intelligence officer under NATO's Kosovo Force [KFOR] in 2003–2004.) What follows here are selections from the *Kabul Kurier* that capture the highlights (and occasional low moments) of my deployment. I hope this book might prove of value to anyone who cares about Afghanistan in particular, or simply wants to pick up lessons on how to approach the challenge of getting to know an unfamiliar culture.

When the smoke clears a bit in Afghanistan and this current dreadful chapter is finally behind us, I dearly hope the world will work together to find a successful long-term approach to help the people of that beleaguered nation to build a better and more inclusive future while continuing to honor, preserve and treasure the best of its dramatic and storied past.

—Brigadier General (Ret) Peter B Zwack
Former Director of the Joint Intelligence and
Operations Center Afghanistan (JIOC-A)
Wilson Center Global Fellow–The Kennan Institute

KABUL KURIER PART I

ARRIVAL

This is our house, the home of lions and tigers

We will beat everyone who attacks us

We are the defenders of our great country

—Popular song written by Afghan singer Siraji
addressed to the Taliban

June 6, 2008

THE LAST RAYS OF SUN were long gone by the time the small C-21 jet I was aboard touched down on the tarmac of the sprawling U.S. military airfield at Bagram, Afghanistan. The 3,000-mile flight from Heidelberg, Germany, already felt like a dream. Even before the jet's engines shut down, the comfort and serenity of the past few hours vanished, replaced by heavy flak vests, helmets, and the roar of fully-armed and blacked-out Blackhawk helicopters from the 101st Air Assault Division. As we hopped aboard the choppers, door gunners stationed themselves at mounted machine guns on each side of the aircraft, on the lookout for insurgent ground fire. Twenty minutes later, we landed at NATO's International Security and Assistance Force (ISAF) Headquarters in Kabul, Afghanistan—my home for the next thirteen months. Tomorrow I would begin my new job as Director of the Joint Intelligence and Operations Center (JIOC-A).

By the time I reached my small room in ISAF's "Ankara" building, it was well past midnight. I took time to set up my bedding and then began my ritual of writing a diary page and saying the Lord's Prayer before going to bed. I unpacked my little daughter's "Twinkle Twinkle Little Star" Winnie-the-Pooh stuffed animal and her favorite stuffed Steiff giraffe that she gave me for good luck before I departed. (The giraffe sleeps under my pillow.) It was a bit surreal to think that just a few hours earlier, at the U.S. military base in Heidelberg, I had kissed my wife Stephanie and our three children goodbye—knowing that we would probably not see one another for at least six months.

Every night, whatever the hour and wherever I am, I follow the same bedtime routine that I created during my year in the Balkans at Kosovo in 2003 and 2004. I learned then that having a routine—including making my bed every morning—is essential for one's state of mind, especially when virtually every day is a jumbled, often discordant series of loosely connected events. I knew Kabul would be no different. After whispering the Lord's Prayer, I put on my "Chill Out 'Sofa Beat' Tunes" CD, which I bought in Skopje in 2003 and played every night in Kosovo. Then I plugged in my cell phone to charge overnight.

Leaving for Afghanistan felt quite different from my departure for Kosovo in the war-torn Balkans five years earlier. Although we were naturally sad and a bit apprehensive about my new assignment, we felt less uncertainty this time as a family. We were now "veterans" and understood what we were facing. The Zwack clan was also spread out around the globe; my deployment to Afghanistan would not feel quite so "foreign" and far-off as Kosovo had in 2003. Two of my children, Broghan and Peter Jr., were older and embarking on first-time "deployments" of their own to boarding schools. My younger daughter Alessandra would remain with my wife in Heidelberg, on the army base that had been our home for two years.

Trying to settle my overactive brain so I could fall asleep, I thought about the day's travels. I had accompanied a senior general officer from Ramstein Air Base in Germany. The flight was a fast-paced journey through Time. Our trajectory carried us over hallowed grounds of antiquity in mere hours; it took Alexander the Great months and years to march across the same terrain. As we headed into Istanbul, Turkey (formerly named Constantinople), to refuel, we could easily spot the crablike shapes of the Blue Mosque (finished in 1616) and the Byzantine Hagia Sophia (built-in 537 CE) in the sprawling and ancient cityscape. Traces of battered walls and other fortification landmarks were a reminder that Constantinople had once controlled land and sea access between Europe and Asia. I could conjure up images of the ferocity and desperation of Constantinople's great siege defense against the invading Ottomans, the grand city finally falling in an orgy of blood and sacking in 1453. (Read Roger Crowley's *Constantinople: The Last Great Siege* for a splendid account of this epic battle.)

We then flew over historic Anatolia and, after cresting the formidable Caucasus Mountains, crossed miles of flat, arid land before landing in the oil depot city of Baku, Azerbaijan, to take on yet more fuel. The sight of Baku from the air reminds me of Rube Goldberg—the urban landscape is a logic-defying visual puzzle of oil pipeline infrastructure galloping off in every direction. After crossing the shallow, turquoise blue Caspian Sea, we flew to the south, skirting Iran and passing over Pakistan, before setting course directly for mountain-girdled Bagram.

And now here I was, in the wee hours, in a strange bed in a strange land, trying to get a little shut-eye before plunging into my new assignment.

The following morning, as I made my way to my first meetings at ISAF headquarters, I was greeted by a somber sight: a parade of forty colorful international flags fluttering at half-mast. The lowered flags signaled that a member of the NATO-led coalition in Afghanistan—the one I now belonged to—had recently died.

An hour later, I was at my desk, ready to get to work.

ISAF HQ: The Routine

October 25, 2008

LIFE HERE IS TOLERABLE, THOUGH the grind is relentless and endless. I am the Director of the Joint Intelligence and Operations Center Afghanistan (JIOC-A) on the NATO ISAF Headquarters in Kabul. My office is not far from Massoud Circle. Nearby, in March 2007, a car bomb spewed its terrible cargo, killing and maiming dozens of hapless Kabul citizens who were simply in the wrong place at the wrong time.

Three weeks ago, a rocket landed about two hundred meters from our compound, waking everyone up and sending us to the bunkers. This has happened twice during the five months I have been here— both times on significant days to the Afghans—and appears to be a crude but effective kinetic "calling card" to remind one and all that the insurgents and terrorists can reach inside Kabul, the capitol city, at will. The sheer inaccuracy of these 107mm rockets is what makes them most disconcerting—we have no clue where they will land, making their strikes equivalent to the Russian roulette of being struck by lightning.

The first rocketing was the night after "National Day," the annual commemoration of the Tajik Warlord and General Ahmad Massoud, killed by a suicide attacker just two days before 9/11. An insurgent disguised as a camera operator had been able to get close to the Tajik leader to assassinate him. To this day, speculation runs rife about whether the attack was happenstance timing or the prequel to the 9/11 attacks in the United States.

The JIOC-A runs a 24/7 intelligence watch and analysis operation, with day and night shifts, ensuring that the day's work is never-ending and never complete. I belong to a U.S. operation linked to Central Command back in Tampa, Florida, but I also have British, Australians, Canadians, and a New Zealander nested comfortably in our midst. Our group numbers about 130 souls, split between Kabul and Kandahar. We are a mix of Army, Air Force, Navy, and Marines, with many civilian inter-agency experts and the allies (mentioned above) augmenting us. All arrive at separate times for different tour lengths—four or six months or a year, which raises hell with nailing down any consistency and coherency to our rotations, pre-deployment training, scheduling, or long-term continuity.

I would be "sunk" and would "crash"—to borrow nautical and aviation terms—without the U.S. Navy and Air Force because they provide the bulk of my personnel and analysts. (Author's note: the bulk of deployed Army military intelligence personnel were commited to Iraq.)

For the Navy, the closest thing to water in the Kabul area is the mostly dried-up Kabul River and the nearby Surobi Dam. Earlier this summer, local insurgents ambushed a small ISAF French Detachment, inflicting heavy losses in the Uzbin Valley in the Surobi District.

Afghanistan indeed has been an "economy of force" operation since 2003, especially for the U.S. Army that has, and continues to have, the overwhelming bulk of its forces in Iraq. I love my people—I do—they represent the best our nation can offer. Many are reservists from multiple levels of society, including a financial analyst from Wall Street, an industrial engineer from Maine, and two schoolteachers. I call this hard-working aggregate of intelligent souls our "Little Engine that Could" because I am daily amazed at what they produce, considering that most had never imagined, even a year ago, that they would be serving in Afghanistan.

For the Americans working these long days, it is frustrating that we are "dry"—meaning, no alcohol—on a compound where all of our NATO allies can have some beer or wine to relax whenever the day ends, but we cannot. This Puritan work ethic can be demanding for my hard-working soldiers, sailors, airmen, marines, and civilians who trudge out the door at work's end only to see NATO personnel having a "cold one" before calling it a night.

This discrepancy in time, commitment, and mission focus were particularly visible during last summer's European Cup (soccer). For over a month, most European contingents at ISAF donned their national sports uniforms. They played their own European Cup here, a contest won by the plucky Macedonians who provide the ISAF compound's security force. How our world has changed! I do not begrudge these activities, as I am hugely committed to NATO and the importance of coalitions, but in our little world here in Kabul, the differences among our various cultures are stark.

I arise around 05:45, and my workday starts at about 06:45, and rarely do I depart my humble little basement office before 10:30–11:00 p.m. and often later. Mostly I crave satisfying sleep. Work and emails pile up at day's end because I try to manage by "walking around" rather than being office-centric. That means that items needing my attention are waiting on my desk "after hours." That is just the way it is—after all, Washington, DC, is awake and spinning at that time, just when we're ready to call it a day in Kabul.

Every day here is different. We try to build predictability around a framework of multiple meetings and office calls but rarely succeed. The only predictable thing here—and in insurgencies, in general—is guaranteed unpredictability in the who, what, where, when, and why (the so-called 5 Ws), except in rare circumstances when intelligence gets the jump on an enemy. Any work toward establishing a norm is usually interrupted by incidents that pop up almost hourly nationwide. When I get back to my little room—a blessed sanctuary with an Internet drop—I try some nights to "Skype" Stephanie and the kids. What a fantastic innovation Skype is.

After my complete hip replacement almost two years ago, I've learned to run again—or, more accurately, practice a fast shuffle. I move at a slight list to my right as the surgery by a superb German doctor took about 8 millimeters more bone out of my right femur— nothing that a small neoprene insert can't fix. Being able to jog again has done legions for my morale because, while I can work out on an elliptical trainer, I vastly prefer being outside, seeing what I can of our dusty little world on our tight compound. Moving in this way is mental and physical oxygen for me, as I thought I would never be able to run freely outside again.

Health wise, I have generally been OK too, although I've had two nasty bouts with the famed Kabul "crud" that had me prostrate and emitting north and south for short, intense, and uncomfortable 24-hour periods. I do not know how it came, via food or by stomach flu, but it certainly was no fun. My lower back also seized up for about a 72-hour period, something that had never happened before. The Flexeril prescribed to me put me into a legal three-day daze!

All this, except for the illness bouts, has been rather rewarding in a somewhat masochistic way. It's the culmination of over 27 years working in the U.S. Army as a tactical and strategic intelligence officer and a Eurasian Foreign Area Officer with a Russian focus. And now, here I am in Afghanistan, a country that most of our NATO allies believe is worth supporting, despite some parliamentary dustups.

ECHOES FROM KOSOVO

THE LONGER I AM HERE, the more I realize that my endless year in Kosovo helped hardwire my brain for the even more rigorous challenges of serving as an intelligence officer in Afghanistan. In a lower density and less-lethal way (I was there in 2003–2004), the intrigues, criminality, corruption, and clan structures in Kosovo allowed me to quickly assimilate to the macro issues of Afghanistan. The overwhelming flood of data points here—the dozens of tribes and sub-tribes, the various ethnic and insurgent groups, warlords, and their political and local agendas—makes it devilishly complex to learn, let alone master, the threat and environment here.

In addition, the dangerously unstable Pakistan dimension—the real strategic concern of this region—also plagues much of what we do to counter the insurgency in Afghanistan. The porous border with Iran also remains an irritant. Still, Iranian money and investment in Afghanistan's western region do as much good for the economy and stability of the Herat area as some of Iran's more under-handed activities.

While this country and its citizens are very pious in religious terms, the internecine warfare takes on a different flavor here—more ethnic than religious. Except for the Mongol-descended Shiite Hazara, who constitute about ten percent of the population, most of the other Muslims here are Sunni. The more extremist Sunnis aim their bile at the "infidel" foreign NATO "occupation" forces and negative, non-traditional Afghan Western and globalist influences they (we) represent.

However, Sunni extremism—as practiced by the Taliban—is generally not welcome throughout Afghanistan. The country had its "Muslim fundamentalist moment" under the Taliban government from 1996 to 2001. The bulk of independent-minded Afghans did not enjoy the experience. If you have not already done so, read or see Khaled Hosseini's *The Kite Runner* to get the flavor of the culture and the time. Two other books that I strongly recommend—written by adventurous female journalists who dig deep into the soul of Afghanistan's male-dominated society—are *The Punishment of Virtue* by Sarah Chayes and *The Sewing Circles of Herat* by Christina Lamb.

Chayes, who still lives in Kandahar and runs a high-quality, fruit-based soap cooperative with local women, is interesting to talk to. She is an expatriate with deep personal knowledge of Afghanistan's nuances. Additionally, I also recommend reading Pakistani author Ahmed Rashid's *The Taliban*, which gives superb background and insight into the details of pre-9/11 Afghanistan and Pakistan— essential to understanding the overall situation here. His current 2008 tome *Descent into Chaos* begins with the post-9/11 U.S. and NATO intervention in the region, up to the current complex situation.

BRIEF DETOUR:
A PRIMER ON AFGHANISTAN

I THINK A SHORT PRIMER on Afghanistan would be a good thing
right about now.

Afghanistan is truly the crossroads of South-Central Asia. Great
trading routes—including the legendary Silk Road—as well as
numerous invasion routes have crisscrossed this region north and
south of the formidable Hindu-Kush mountains that extend into
central Afghanistan from the Himalayas.

The highest peak in Afghanistan is Noshaq, which rises to over
24,000 feet, just a few thousand less than Mt. Everest and K2. Almost
everything related to commerce and urban living in Afghanistan
occurs on the lowland at the base of the mountains, areas linked
by the thin reed of Highway 1 that snakes around these formidable
peaks.

Foreign expeditions into this region during ancient times are legendary. These include Alexander the Great and his Greek coalition, whose truly extraordinary foray twenty-four centuries ago can still be seen at the complex of ruins at Balkh, near Mazar. He is said to have captured and married the Persian Princess Roxana in 327 BCE during his conquest; today, the light-colored eyes and fair complexions of residents in remote and dangerous Nuristan are considered proof of the union. (In 1985, *National Geographic* magazine captivated the world with a cover photo of a 17-year-old Pashtun woman with startlingly light eyes. When the magazine found her again in 2002, that striking young lady had weathered and aged markedly in a scant 17 years!)

Almost two thousand years after Alexander's incursion, the powerful Persian (Iranian) Safavids conquered and held huge swaths of southwest Asia, including Afghanistan. The Persian influence is particularly evident in Herat, the loveliest and most stable city in Afghanistan. (Perhaps coincidentally, Herat is also where resistance to the Soviet 1979–1989 occupation of Afghanistan took root.)

Long before the military campaigns of Alexander and the Safavids, Afghanistan felt the foreign influence of another kind: Buddhism. More than two thousand years ago, Buddhist culture filtered into the country and became part of the landscape, literally.

Early Buddhists built the extraordinary twin sculptures at Bamian that were blown up by the Taliban in March 2001. The ancient statues were deemed idolatrous by Mullah Omar, the six-foot, six-inch tall, one-eyed Amirul Momineen "Commander of the Faithful." Omar overplayed his hand. The callous destruction of one of the Buddhist world's most hallowed legacies convinced even the most ardent apologists for the Taliban that the regime was unbelievably weird, pre-medieval, and totally disconnected from the rest of our evolving world.

As you can see, to truly understand modern Afghanistan requires an appreciation of the central role that geography plays in its history. The nation's location exposed it to many positive cultural influences, expressed in beautiful architecture, art, cuisine, and more across the centuries. But, as I've pointed out, it also made Afghanistan vulnerable to invasion. Arguably the most catastrophic incursion was that of the fearsome Mongols who swept through the region in the early 1200s CE, laying waste to great cities and cultural centers such as ancient Balkh. These nomads were the medieval equivalent of an atomic bomb; their arrival in any area generally presaged the extinction of the local culture and the people.

The encroachments and invasions of the past two millennia

explain in part the emergence of Afghanistan's hardy and fanatically independent mountain and valley folk. Driven into the highland fastnesses for survival from the lowlands and cities, the people created tightly-knit communities as protection against intruders—including neighbors just one valley over. The resulting inbreeding created tribes, sub-tribes, and clans that constantly warred with one another unless faced by a common foe. The Appalachian "Hatfields and McCoys" were minor leagues compared to these fearsome, proud, brave, generous, hospitable, but also vengeful mountain clans that have terrorized a succession of invaders and lowlands people over the centuries.

Suspicious of central government and xenophobic to the extreme, the existence of these insular tribes and clans explains in part the complex nature of the primarily Pashtun insurgency we are facing today. Further complicating things is the sheer geographical remoteness and compartmentalization of these groups. Being cut off from the larger world enhances the power of village elders and supplies fertile ground for charismatic proselytizers of religious piety, such as some Muslim Mullahs. Finally, physical isolation, combined with centuries of aversion to outside influence, greatly retard education, especially of females. Today, the literacy rate in many remote highland regions is not more than 20 percent of the men and less than ten percent of women.

Altogether, these factors create a huge challenge: How do the Government of the Islamic Republic of Afghanistan (GIRoA), the ISAF, and the United Nations (through non-governmental organizations or NGOs) reach these people with their message

COMPETING ETHNICITIES

FOR OUTSIDERS, SORTING THROUGH AFGHANISTAN'S hundreds of tribes and sub-tribes is a seemingly impossible task. The easiest place to begin is the six major ethnic groups that comprise this nation. The dominant **Pashtuns** constitute approximately 42 percent of Afghanistan's roughly 32 million population and are the majority ethnic group in today's insurgency. (I will write more about the Pashtuns later.)

Next are the **Tajiks**, who comprise about 27 percent of Afghanistan's population. Traditionally no friend of the Pashtuns, Tajiks are grouped primarily in the North around Mazar-al-Sharif. They became famous for their epic—and successful—defense against multiple failed Soviet armored assaults into their Panjshir Valley stronghold near Bagram in the 1980s.

Four more distinct ethnic groups make up the rest of the population: **Uzbeks** (9 percent,) **Hazara** (9 percent), **Turkmen**

(3 percent), and **Baluchis** (2 percent). Two other tiny groups are also worth mentioning: Nuristanis, who have links to Alexander the Great (100,000), and the nomadic Kuchis of Pashtun ethnicity.

Notably, only the Hazara, who descend directly from the fearsome Mongols, are Shiite Muslims. The rest of the population is predominantly Sunni. Religious-based civil war, as we experienced in Iraq, is not likely in Afghanistan. Instead, conflict grows out of ethnic and tribal rivalries. (That said, all Sunni ethnicities tend to pick on the Shiite Hazaras—often viciously.)

It was into this spicy stew that the British leaped in 1838, having pushed northwest from their Indian territories to build a buffer zone against the Russians—the centerpiece of the so-called Great Game. By 1842 this first expedition turned into an unmitigated disaster for the British. Feisty Afghanistan—sandwiched between competing forces in the north (Russia) and south (Britain)—showed its spiny side to all parties. (More on this later.)

It's worth noting that the formidable British prevailed almost everywhere for centuries in their colonial endeavor except in the American colonies and Afghanistan.

For fun, I've laid out the Alphabet and some associated words about Afghanistan. Google the terms and topics to learn more about this strange and unique place.

Alphabet about Afghanistan

A is for Afghanistan and the Argandab

B is for Bagram and Baitullah

C is for Chapan

D is for Durrani and Dadullah

E is for Elphinstone

F is for FATA and Faisabad

G is for Gandamak and Ghilzai

H is for Herat and Haqqani

I is for Islamabad and Ismail Khan

J is for Jalalabad, and Jezail

K is for Kabul and Kandahar, Khyber, Karzai and Khost

L is for Loya Jirga (Grand Council) and Lashkar Gah

M is for Mullah Omar, Mazar, Maiwand & Martini Henry

N is for Nuristan and Nahrin

O is for Osama and Opium

P is for Poppy and Pashtunwali

Q is for QRF (Quick reaction force) and Qalat

R is for Rabbani and Ramadan

S is for Shindand and Shura

T is for Taliban

U is for Uruzgan

V is for Vizier

W is for Waziristan and Wardak

X is for Xenophobia (a common Afghan trait)

Y is for Yahya Khel

Z is for Zawahiri, Zabul, and Zadran Arc

THE COALITION CHALLENGE

October 25, 2008, diary entry

IN MY CURRENT ROLE AS the JIOC-A Director, I am also a NATO Deputy Intelligence officer (Deputy CJ2). My job involves exchanging and disseminating intelligence information and coordination among our many Allies here in Kabul and across the country.

For instance, there are 14 National Intelligence Cells (NICs) here on the Kabul ISAF compound alone. These NICs support the national contingents, in this case, primarily the U.S., Polish, and French in the East, but also British, Australians, Dutch, and Canadians in the heavily stressed South; Italians, and Spanish in the increasingly dangerous West; and Germans, Norwegians, Danes and Swedes in the relatively quiet North. I've even met and visited a Hungarian contingent here.

Every week I sit in meetings with all these Allies where, as best we can, we share our observations and perspectives on everything happening around the country. For intelligence cooperation and diplomacy, this regular gathering is particularly important. Aggressive "American exceptionalism" can unintentionally jangle Allies' sensibilities and create resentment toward the U.S. I work this relationship-building hard.

Although I'm usually chained all day to the computer terminals and feeds in our JIOC-A dungeon, I push to get out to see the land first-hand. *Without doing so, my analysis and assessments will be tainted by a conjured-up fantasy about what I think I am seeing.* In late spring, after numerous delays, we will move into a new state-of-the-art facility that I might enjoy for a month before departing.

Frankly, it is incredible how technology and bandwidth have expanded to pass data. We now face the dilemma of information overload. The challenge is to put the info into context. How does it fit with what we know of the "cultural terrain"? How does it dovetail with the ethnicities and tribes, the customs, and regional neighbors?

This is no small thing. It is essential to *know* a place and a people, not simply imagine what they're like. Without context, you risk missing the texture and granularity of key intelligence reads. I speak as an old Foreign Area Officer who often gets out to see and experience quite a bit of local life in interesting regions of the world. Protecting our forces and facilities is certainly critical, but it can make on-the-ground exploration difficult. I seize every opportunity to get away from ISAF headquarters to see the lay of the land and to meet and talk to Afghans of all ethnicities and tribes. Regrettably, I don't speak Dari or Pashtun. Among older citizens and Afghan officers, I can use my Russian. Otherwise, I simply have to use my eyes and long experience in foreign lands to absorb what I see.

Next are a few vignettes from times when I've been able to leave HQ behind and explore. My excursions have mainly been in and around the greater Kabul area.

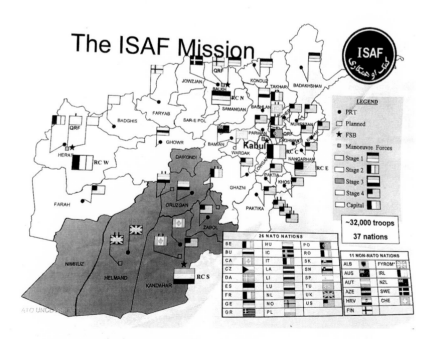

TRIP TO PUL-E-CHARKHI PRISON

As some of you have read in the press, there has been a lot of trouble at the Pul-e-Charkhi Prison in a remote location west of Kabul, off the road to Jalalabad and the Khyber Pass. Journalist and activist Ann Jones's sobering book *Kabul in Winter: Life Without Peace* (2006) prominently featured the women's block of this notorious prison.

One morning, we drove out to the prison in an unobtrusive SUV to check out the surroundings. We set out in civilian clothes, with colorful local scarves draped over our protective vests just to look a little less military. We all carried Beretta pistols, and an M4 automatic rifle sat low along the vehicle's floorboard.

As always, the goal when traveling like this is to make the operator of a Remote Control or Command wire improvised explosive device (IED) look twice before he hits the button or plunger. By the time he makes up his mind—at least in theory—we will have driven past

33

the blast zone. The same goes for a vehicle-borne suicide bomber. When we go off-compound in full military garb, we look like the equivalent of those armored "Teenage Mutant Ninja Turtles"— trussed up Agincourt-style in forty pounds of protective gear and body armor. What a sight we must present to the locals or even to the expats who wander downtown. Sadly, this get-up hasn't always been our custom. ISAF soldiers could move around in a lower, more relaxed profile in the early days of the mission. Today, the insurgency is more widespread and dangerous.

The drive west out of Kabul that morning was along a serviceable road that bustled with activity. Vendors of every ethnicity—Tajik, Hazara, some Pashtun—were hawking mostly foodstuffs. An array of fruits, vegetables, and drinks lined the roads, available for purchase. Burqaed mothers led or carried their children, often behind the man of the family. The buff lower mountains of the Kabul Kuhestan range loomed. Before getting close to the foothills, we turned south onto a dreadfully maintained road that led directly to the village of Pul-e-Charkhi.

Suddenly, we felt distinctly different and alone. As we bounced along the severely rutted road, we observed that we were clearly in a Pashtun-dominated area. Faces, turbans, clothing, and demeanor were markedly different from what we were used to seeing in the urban center. We received hard looks from a few younger males— surely some of them were participating in the insurgency or had done so in the past. Older males with distinctive beards and turbans watched us curiously as they sat or lay in the shade on their woven rattan mats and beds.

We pushed through the crowded center of the road, droves of kids peering in our heavily shaded windows, looking for handouts. One enterprising teenager defiantly flipped us off. Up ahead, the road traffic backed up, blocked by three squat, fully armored beige HUMVEEs that gingerly inched their way forward through the kids and narrow streets. You could see that the gunners were nervous. Despite the size of their vehicles, they were totally vulnerable to a close-in grenade or suicide attack. The turrets of these mini-tanks swiveled back and forth to encourage the locals to stay back without success. We were all aliens, infidels, in a truly strange place.

After eventually working our way through the chaotic village, we arrived at the massive prison. It is a vast hulking facility with gray walls and bastions that give it almost a medieval feel. Inside the overcrowded prison, run by the Government of Afghanistan, there are prisoners of every stripe and offense. Within its inner sanctum is a zone filled with barely controlled hard-core Taliban and other insurgents that always make trouble and create dangerous stand-offs for the guard force. The prisons are truly challenged here and are targets in themselves. No doubt many of you read about the June (2008) prison break at Sarpoza near Kandahar, where over nine hundred escaped when an external insurgent force broke into the compound. The daring jailbreak, coupled with significant fighting in nearby Arghandab, kept Kandahar in the global news for over a week.

Short on time, we considered taking a back road to Kabul but prudently decided to push our way through the chaotic village again. (Two weeks later, an IED exploded on the back-road route we had contemplated using, killing one U.S. soldier and wounding another. The attack occurred so close to this village, and it certainly was possible that one of the young men who stared so boldly at us that day was a member of the insurgents who planted the deadly device. The roads in Afghanistan have become ever more dangerous as insurgents have adopted some of the lessons and techniques used in Iraq. You never know when your luck will run out simply by hitting the wrong rut of a dirt road, setting off a gigantic pressure plate mine. Or you might cross a culvert or other spot and be the unwitting target of a command wire or remote-control device. Most of our soldiers are killed by these insidious devices. To boot, many suicide attackers in Afghanistan have become more imaginative in their efforts to join Allah in Paradise by foot, vehicle, and even bicycle. For the soldiers driving all day in the hinterland, the concentration and relentless effort needed to avoid hitting an IED—one that can easily blow up even an up-armored HUMVEE—have to be unbearably stressful day-in and day-out.

The Less Fortunate

WHEN POSSIBLE, I'VE JOINED THE occasional humanitarian and goodwill missions that ISAF sometimes conducts in Kabul. One rare opportunity was a visit to a very depressed Afghan refugee camp to the West of Kabul, in formerly peaceful Wardak Province. With nowhere to go, these unfortunates—over five thousand strong— were the human detritus of thirty years of war and strife. From the late 1970s until now (2008), over six million people were uprooted in Afghanistan, first by the Soviets, then by civil war, and more recently by the Taliban.

We arrived in a convoy of nine SUVs at what appeared to be a sea of long, flat, bleached-out tents that stretched hundreds of yards in all directions. The kids, some boys almost naked, came running from all directions. Girls, too, some dressed in their best colorful finery and slathered in cheap lipstick, also approached us, but the boys and men were more aggressive. Bearded and wizened village elders with distinctive turbans and flat Pakul hats tried to keep order, employing canes and sticks to ward off a growing mob that engulfed our convoy.

As we began to pass out items to the crowd, the good-natured group became more frantic to get the clothes and other goods. I handed fistfuls of confections from a huge candy bag to the kids, and in no time a dozen little hands were in my bag, forcing me to let it go. It was the same with clothes. The mass pressed closer—well-meaning but desperate—and made it impossible to hand out individual items to individual people. Older men came away with infant toys, and children hauled away adult shirts and pants. Shoes were particularly popular—everything from Kmart sandals to Disney princess slippers to Lands' End moccasins came flying out of the boxes. I sure hope the Camp got everyone together afterward to match all the single shoes that we could not hand out in pairs due to the pressing, grasping human throng. Finally after about 20 minutes we departed; our supplies were depleted. Many waved goodbyes, others stared, and a few glowered. I wonder what will happen to them and the hundreds of other refugee camps around the country when winter comes.

A few weeks later, we visited a school for Hazara boys. The school was a rundown cluster of classrooms in a low-slung building that looked quite open to the elements. Inside were spartan classrooms where strong-willed women in scarves but no veil or burqa conducted their classes on old chalkboards. Encouraging to see was that all were working on reading skills. The young boys, all with crew-cuts, were reasonably well-dressed and tried so hard to behave when we entered the classrooms with donated bags and boxes of mostly school supplies—everything from notebooks and rulers to crayons and pencils. Simply saying "Nâmêtân cist" (what's your name?) was enough to break the ice (we were in our heavy armored gear), and the kids broke into huge grins, dark eyes a'sparklin' at the prospect of receiving some items. At first, they waited in a patient line. However, all control was lost when a soccer ball came out of a bag. It was a friendly but chaotic moment, as many are in Afghanistan. I would like to think that some soon-to-be young men remember well the Americans and other foreigners who visited their classrooms.

EXTRAORDINARY WOMEN

I was a young girl in a place where women were regarded as property along

with gold and land—the three zs of the Pashtuns,

zan, zar, and zamin

—and kept hidden away behind curtained doorways.

-Christina Lamb, journalist, 1998

ANOTHER ENCOUNTER I HAD WAS a birthday party at the home of an expatriate Afghan woman who adopted little girls and raised them as her own family. She had seven when we visited her, and it was the birthday of three of them. The exact date of their birthdays didn't matter. The fact was that they were getting loving attention from this extraordinary woman, who had been a Deputy in one of Karzai's ministries, and her close-knit group of friends. It was a labor of love for her, spiced with poignancy as several teenagers that she had raised

43

as her children had been "reclaimed" by their families for unpopular arranged marriages, a common cultural practice here. (Read Khaled Hosseini's beautiful *A Thousand Splendid Suns* for an achingly moving portrayal of a woman's life in traditional Afghanistan.)

Among this woman's friends was a young Tajik man who I was pointedly told represented Afghanistan's future. He had become the head of Afghanistan's Chamber of Commerce, which had more than five thousand members subscribed. We talked at length about how the post-Taliban period had begun with such optimism but then quickly deteriorated. The situation had only worsened during the past three years. He all but implored me to push the Government of Afghanistan and the International Community to come up with ways, any ways, to find employment for the 100,000s of young military-age Afghan males who could contribute positively to Afghanistan's economy if given an alternative to the drug trade or insurgency. If only they could find a meaningful job to support themselves and their families. As a young entrepreneur, he spoke of the oppressive, pervasive corruption from the highest government to the lowest local cop that resulted in taxes and demands for protection money to ensure that businesses were protected. One unintended consequence of this negative activity was thousands of possible recruits for the Taliban.

Another young man at the party worked for one of Afghanistan's telecommunications companies. He described how he received intimidation telephone calls nightly from the Taliban, who threatened him unless service was turned off. Earlier in the year, there was a rash of telephone cell towers attacked in insurgency-dominated areas. A family man, he talked about how he used to drive out with his wife and kids into adjoining Wardak and Logar Provinces or north toward the scenic Panjshir Valley on an enjoyable Friday outing. Given the increasing and random attacks by insurgents and criminals along many of the region's roads, he is afraid to do so now. Clean-shaven, he also mentioned that he liked to wear a jacket and tie, which today could get him killed in the more remote countryside.

The four women I met at the party were particularly impressive. All were entrepreneurs, two of whom had been in government within the Ministry of Finance. There are fewer women today in Ministries than were present during the more optimistic years of 2003–4. All were thoroughly modern in a Western sense and swam upstream against Afghanistan's retrograde cultural climate, especially in areas outside the cities. One enterprising woman owned several businesses and trained women for careers in industry. She proudly told me how she had taught over five thousand women for vocational jobs in

Kabul. During the repressive Taliban period (1996–2001), she ran an underground clothing factory that employed over 250 women directly under the regime's nose. So loyal were her workers and their families, including men, no one turned her into the Taliban "purity police."

She and her cohorts all acknowledged that they could not travel freely in most of the country anymore. As liberated Afghan women, society was not ready to absorb them. It will take years and years.

After we departed, it struck me that we almost always meet with the men here—many of whom are corrupt—and that we rarely interface with the women who, more than anyone, see the adverse effects of corruption. And who lose their young, impressionable, oft-unemployed sons to the Taliban or the Afghan Security Forces, where many are killed. There must be a way to better leverage over 50 percent of Afghanistan's population toward building a more positive living and working environment here.

Naive thoughts on my part, perhaps? To the minds of many Afghans, 85 percent of whom live in a mostly rural, often violent fundamentalist culture—such notions threaten the very heart of their culture and religion.

9/11 Full Circle in Afghanistan

THE FOLLOWING IS AN EXCERPT of a note I recently sent to friends and family commemorating the September 11, 2001, attacks in the United States. I wanted to include it in this memoir to capture what I felt on this solemn day in Afghanistan. I am sending U.S. flags we had that day in Kabul to the two schools that most formed me, Fessenden in Massachusetts and Trinity in New York City, so that their young students will never forget the significance of that day.

"This is just a brief note from the ISAF Headquarters in Kabul, Afghanistan, where at 6:07 p.m., about a hundred of us assembled in front of our American flag that fluttered at half-mast to commemorate the 9/11 attack against the United States. Fittingly, this commemoration was in the heart of the country from which al-Qaeda seven years ago conceived, planned, and enabled this horrific act and, in doing so, decisively changed the fabric of the world. A bell gonged for each of the military and

DoD civilians who died that morning in the Pentagon. Prayer is also said for all the other innocents of many nations who went about their unsuspecting everyday routines that beautiful Tuesday morning in New York City, Washington DC, or on Flight 93."

It is here that I shall end this first edition of the *Kabul Kurier*. Reading it over, I can see it is a bit disjointed due to all the starts and stops I have had to make while writing it over the past three months (June to October 2008).

Suffice it to say: We have our work cut out over here in this stunning but violent land. We are far from achieving lasting, permanent success in helping to provide credible governance, perceived fairness in the rule of law, and improved quality of life for most Afghans here, whatever their ethnicity. An active internal and external insurgency—exported mainly from Pakistan—works hard to subvert our progress and gains. At the same time, continued high production and processing of opium into heroin corrodes and corrupts all levels of Afghan society and helps fuel the insurgency.

Still, I've met many Afghan people who are worthy of our continued presence and nation-building. They are brave and proud; for many, honor is their most precious possession. Working here, however, requires a deft touch. While retaliation for 9/11 brought us here, we (the U.S. and our allies) are now also involved in a nation-building endeavor from which we simply cannot walk away. We withdrew once before when the Soviets were defeated in 1989 after a decade of trying to conquer Afghanistan. The country and the region sank into chaos from which a dangerous, exported malignancy arose to strike us.

While simultaneously building the basis for good governance, this mission to defeat the insurgency will take years to achieve. Not continuing with this endeavor will bring even more internal Afghan grief and suffering and likely continued turmoil in nuclear armed Pakistan, which could spawn even more dangerous transnational threats in the uncertain future.

UH-60 Blackhawks flying in tandem and overwatch over rugged Afghan terrain.

Pictures Section I

Traditional Islamic mosque meets the hubbub of Kabul's streets and citizenry.

Traditional burqa woman wearing high heels.

Alert HUMVEE convoy in Pul-e-Charkhi village—note gunner in cupola is facing the vehicle's rear.

The grim looking Pul-e-Charki prison on the outskirts of Kabul.

Afghan security team heading toward Massoud Circle in Kabul, site of grisly suicide bombing in 2007.

Arrival at a refugee camp in Wardak Province southwest of Kabul—excited little Afghan tykes mobbing one of our SUVs looking for candy and gifts.

Heart-melting, this little girl is holding stuffed animals handed out by our team.

Knee-high, mingling with both exuberant and shy Afghan boys and girls.

A traditional Afghan family—man in front with wife and child behind.

One wonders what this young boy's hard eyes have seen in his short life.

An old-world Afghan patriarch outside Kabul whose extended family and clan have likely endured little but conflict and tragedy since 1979.

Stalwarts of my JIOC-A team on a rooftop at ISAF headquarters 2009.

Hoisting Old Glory on the 4th of July.

KABUL KURIER PART II

Diary Entries from
October 2008–April 2009

Look into the eyes of an Afghan, and you will see Thirty years
of war, hardship, and suffering

Time is blazing by in my Afghanistan deployment. This edition
of the *Kabul Kurier* will cover from October 2008 to January 2009.
At that point, my ISAF (International Security and Assistance Force)
deployment was briefly interrupted by a required ten-week course at
the Joint Forces Staff College in Norfolk, Virginia, which is where
I am finishing this installment.

There is much to transmit since the last edition (October
2008) of the *Kurier*. This stint was a busy period operationally and
personally, as I shall recount. My knowledge of this multi-nuanced
mission continues to grow and sharpen. Every day, I am reminded
of how little I know of a region and culture to which historians,
archaeologists, and anthropologists have committed lifetimes of

research. My orientation and interest are also evolving from the original bread-and butter threats, security challenges, and issues that are my core competency to the intricate and Byzantine governance issues at the heart of the profound conundrum we are in here. While I spend about ninety percent of my long working day in the dungeon that we call the JIOC-A, I mostly write about the other ten percent of my time because it is the best way to give you the perspective and texture to understand this region and the critical mission we are all charged to undertake here.

As I mentioned in the last *Kurier*, our leadership understands we can't fight our way out of this hydra-headed insurgency. The core issue from my perspective is how the very insular and conservative people in Afghanistan's remote villages and rugged valleys perceive central Afghan governance. Do they see it as fair? Do they see it as credible?

Suppose the Kabul-centric government presence *is* legitimate (which will be no mean feat) and suppose that legitimacy plays out in "deeds not words" that satisfy even a naturally suspicious rural population. In that case, this endeavor may indeed succeed if we set realistic and attainable goals and then depart. But we must also be willing to recognize that this traumatized country will never become a Jeffersonian democracy or significantly change its culture or religion.

We can shape and influence, but the mainstream will not move from moderate Sharia nor is particularly interested in women's rights. The best we can do is influence and soften the rougher edges of these cultural attributes, but it will take generations to change them substantially. What is clear now, in 2009, is that the bulk of the Afghan population does not want to return to ultra-conservative Taliban-Wahhabist-al-Qaeda style Sharia.

If instead of being viewed as credible and fair, the Afghan government is seen by many as corrupt and rapacious, we are in for a more prolonged insurgency. The government official at the village-local town level is an Afghan National Policeman or local politician or bureaucrat that the people see daily. The individual choices and actions of these government representatives can pour fuel on or dampen an insurgency.

The tricky thing for our military coalition is to be conscious of whether we are perceived as partners of an increasingly progressive government or are we seen as foreign agents of an unpopular, opportunistic, and remote Kabul-based entity that perpetuates patronage and local favoritism among various tribes and groups. Add to the mix a poppy-based economy that promotes opportunism and stokes violence.

The good news is that the key international military and political leaders involved in this major endeavor in Afghanistan recognize the obstacles to creating credible governance. They're willing to take substantial steps to build better bridges between Kabul and villages and valleys. Positive governance can take root only with more coordinated community-tribal outreach, better disciplined Afghan troops, and honest cops.

You've possibly read or heard that substantially more reinforcements will arrive this year (2009), which will go a long way to improve the security environment. An improved ability to hold and expand our so-called "security inkblots" will allow these communities to build themselves up, with a lot of UN and NGO assistance. This surge could help pave the way to more stability and an economic future, the bedrock of any stable society.

At the moment, rural Afghanistan has devolved into a nation of "fence-sitters," waiting to see who will prevail—a credible government that provides adequate security, or a return of the Taliban. Other insurgent groups will mete out retaliation and pain to whoever is consorting with the coalition and the government.

This tension between Afghanistan's rural, primarily Pashtun tribal communities and urban Kabul is not new. In 1931, Richard

64

Maconachie, British Minister to Kabul, made the following observation in a dispatch to London. His words still ring true more than three generations later:

"Throughout the country, the advantages of anarchy seem to be better appreciated than its drawbacks. The tribes are asking themselves why they should resign the freedom from which they enjoyed the past year and submit again to a central authority which would inevitably demand payment of land revenue, customs duties, and bribes for its officials and possibly the restoration of arms looted from government posts and arsenals."

With that reality in mind, our main strategic effort in Afghanistan is not just fighting insurgency flare-ups but also providing the security and atmospherics to ensure that a successful and legitimate national election can occur in August (2009). Progress in that direction has been made. After a major four-month-long effort, an Afghan government-led (and ISAF and international community-supported) voter registration effort just concluded in February. It netted success far beyond initial conservative expectations, including within the southern Pashtun belt, where the heart of the insurgency resides. (This is also where the bulk of the well-reported significant U.S. influx of reinforcing troops will deploy this year; Kandahar will be the hub.)

The actual elections scheduled for August will be a major security challenge and will consume our efforts as the day gets close. The elections are critical because—if conducted properly—they will further legitimize the Afghan government in the eyes of the people.

Even with the progress, we see on the election front, it's impossible to ignore the fact that we lost significant time and traction in the early Afghan effort after our focus turned to Iraq in 2003.

We're now trying to make up for that lost time but still face two huge obstacles. One involves the poppy trade. If large-scale opium production continues relatively unabated, illicit funds will continue to corrupt the existing system, undermining governance and fueling various insurgencies, especially the Quetta-based southern Taliban.

When I returned to Kabul in late March after my stint in Norfolk, Virginia, the spring poppy harvest season was about to get underway. This time is a visual treat; fields and hillsides erupt with a red glow as the poppies bloom. Over the course of several months, the harvest moves from north to south, tracking the poppy bloom times. In some parts of the country, the soil is particularly fertile and the weather temperate, allowing for two yields.

Once the harvest is in, thousands of harvesters—mostly younger Pashtun men—will face the choice of unemployment or bearing arms. If they choose the latter option, they pick up Kalashnikovs and RPGs and fight as so-called "$10-a-day Taliban." These young men are not particularly ideological or ultra-pious. Afghanistan is a warrior culture—guns are prized possessions—so it is not a reach for these Pashtuns to jump in with the insurgents for a wide range of reasons, few pertaining to political or religious philosophy.

High unemployment and its relationship to the insurgency need wider publicity. Some legal and policy strides have been undertaken to remove constraints to allow our coalition to deal with the narcotics trade, especially the nexus between insurgents and crooks.

The second key factor that concerns all of us here at ISAF is Pakistan. The country is faced with what it perceives as two existential threats. One is India. Pakistan's nuclear-equipped main-force military is in constant defensive mode toward its equally nuclear-tipped neighbor. At the same time, Pakistan must deal with the growing Taliban-style Islamist insurgency that blossomed unexpectedly and has spread beyond tribal areas into Swat—a former tourist destination dubbed the "Switzerland of Southern Asia," as well as around Peshawar. To boot, Pakistan also must confront a weak economy, high unemployment, poor educational levels, and a volatile political landscape that breeds instability and uncertainty for the entire region.

We must never forget that Afghanistan and Pakistan are inextricably linked. Whatever plays out in Pakistan—not to mention in Iran—will have major effects in Afghanistan. Part of what we see today is the result of actions taken more than a century ago when the 1893 Durand Line—a border agreement between British India and Afghanistan—arbitrarily split many tribes between present-day Afghanistan and Pakistan. No one but the politicians paid much heed to the arbitrary line then or now. Families and tribes simply carried on without missing a beat.

CLOISTERED LIFE ON THE ISAF COMPOUND

EXCEPT FOR MY WORK HOURS and ever-present tension, I live an acceptable life in central Kabul's dusty and small ISAF compound. Since my arrival in June 2008, I've become accustomed to the routine. In our little walled-off cocoon, it is a different world from alien Kabul outside. Except for the occasional escorted Pashtun or Tajik and a few Hazara men workers—easy to identify in their wrapped head scarves—I could be anywhere in the world. The only truly distinctive feature that reminds us daily of where we are is the sound of the Muezzin that calls forth prayers five times a day from a nearby mosque. Of course, the mountains ringing the city also tell me that I'm not at home. As I write this in November, the mountains are topped with frosty crowns of almost blindingly white snow.

The camp we occupy was built on the highland Afghan desert on Kabul's outskirts more than eighty years ago when the city was much smaller. Wolves were said to prowl the area then. The facility was initially an Afghan sporting club established by King Nadir Shah. After his assassination in 1933, it was expanded by his son, the last Afghan King, Zahir Shah, who was named "Father of the Nation" in 2002. Zahir Shah has the rare distinction of being one of only a few Afghan leaders to die of natural causes; he passed away in 2007. With Zahir's passing, the last hopes of returning to some type of benign Afghan ruling monarchy flickered out.

Today, the ISAF compound is highlighted by the distinctive two-storied ochre-colored colonial-style Headquarters building (known by all as the "Yellow Building") where Afghan military and governmental officials used to host large wedding parties. Opposite the HQ, one can get a good cappuccino in the pleasant Destille Garden flanked by a few gift and carpet shops that thrive on coalition dollars and euros. The whole setting is a bit like that movie *The Truman Show*, in that one could live one's entire sojourn in the Camp without knowing or letting the outside world intrude on you ... except when the emergency alert system sounds. It is relatively safe here. That said, I've heard car bombs by day and wildly inaccurate rockets fired by enterprising insurgents at night. We live by the law of percentages here. A rocket will inevitably strike again, at some point, in this very overcrowded little community.

As a student of history, I'm struck by the fact that two thousand four hundred years of history have come full circle here in our little camp. The troops of the Macedonian infantry company that guards us in 2009 are probably descendants of Alexander the Great. The building I live in—the "Ankara Palace"—is a relatively solid two-story concrete structure built by the Turks. Three years before I arrived, it was hit by a rocket. This is why we groggily but dutifully go undercover when the rocket sirens blow and tinny alert PA squawks— almost invariably during the wee hours of the night.

The earthquake tremors we have felt several times almost worry me more. It is a bizarre feeling at, say, 2 a.m., when one is disoriented and suddenly wide-awake, to feel like you are on a waterbed, the slightest little gel wave briefly undulating through and under you.

As I mentioned in the last *Kurier*, I am working with a wonderful cross-section of great Americans from every state in the union, as well as allies and partners from up to forty-two nations. For instance, our inner office boasts a U.S. Navy Lieutenant Commander from Pennsylvania who is my hard-working and ever-patient XO (executive officer). My superb Deputy JIOC-Director and Operations officer, a newly minted Army colonel from Minnesota, came with me last year from Heidelberg. A canny, experienced Vietnam combat veteran is my Senior Advisor and I have the best young senior non-commissioned officer in the U.S. Navy.

The camaraderie, particularly among the one hundred or so soldiers, sailors, Marines, airmen, and civilians in the Kabul JIOC, including Australians, British, and Canadians, is quite good, considering that we were initially squeezed into an extremely small basement facility and work together 24/7. Our tight quarters expanded substantially recently when we moved into a brand spanking-new facility, built by Afghan contractors, who certainly moved at their own pace, far exceeding our original timeline for completion.

While not perfect in its masonry, geometry, and lines, it is a super new building and has greatly improved our capability. Not that the new structure hasn't provided a bit of unwanted excitement, too. Early one gorgeous winter day, we clambered outside to the roof to take in the view, only to see one of our sailors slip and start sliding down the slick triangular structure to certain injury. Fortunately, someone grabbed his wrist as he fell and kept him from plunging over the edge and falling a couple of stories.

I have little to complain about when I compare my berth to soldiers living on the Forward Operating Bases (FOBs). Many of them live with the high tension of being mortared by night and then driving or patrolling in IED-infested areas by day.

As mentioned, the hours are long, with every day bringing a new adventure even during the quieter winter months. I fight to get enough sleep and exercise while trying to eat healthily in the British-run "Supreme" Mess. Much of the service staff are hardworking and mostly genial Indians, so we regularly taste a different curry dish every day. Behind the counter, the Indians keep an extra piquant sauce they apply for themselves.

I am always friendly and polite, which I know they appreciate because not all foreign contingents are courteous to the service staff. In turn, they take good care of me and always find something for me to eat on those occasions when I arrive out-of-breath just after closing time. They also did a marvelous job preparing an exquisite Thanksgiving meal, complete with turkey, stuffing, sweet potatoes, and corn bread—a treat for those of us thousands of miles from home.

In the dining facility, I have to fight the tendency to sit alone and read. The longer my deployment goes on and as more people rotate through, the more reluctant I am to sit down and make an effort to meet new friends, but I generally do.

Maintaining a fitness routine is also a struggle. Still, I generally manage to break out on most days at mid-day for a run-shuffle around camp with my marvelously rebuilt hip. When days get cooler, outdoor running at times becomes questionable. The air then is often fouled with a yellow pumice that includes traces of burnt human excrement—an ingredient used routinely as heating fuel.

Even so, last fall was a gorgeous, almost rain-free "Indian Summer," when I could often run without heavy layers of clothing well into November. The downside was that the fine weather translated into a higher level of insurgent attacks.

After a jog outside, I usually finish up on an elliptical trainer and then stretch while watching sports highlights on ESPN. This activity became especially important to me as we maintained an NFL fantasy "Panjshir Valley Football League," which I somehow won as the "Zwack Attack." All this made the long and late hours of the stressful autumn and early winter more tolerable for a number of our hard-working personnel.

Sleep, exercise, and adequate, balanced nourishment are the three key pillars one must maintain in an environment where the norm is stress and hourly change, and simultaneously demanding high-level analysis and problem-solving. I am relatively unmerciful toward some of my own people who try to "tough out" what I see as excessively long hours, not get exercise, and eat poorly. I require folks to take the leave and passes that they are entitled to by policy and am not impressed when a troop tries to macho their way through our extended mission without taking a break.

My health has been generally good except for another bout with a crud that hit me again in the wee hours that left my system nauseated, drained, exhausted, and crippled by the onset of back spasms that laid me out for a day. This time, I did not like the Flexeril they gave me to cope with the pain; it left me groggy and listless.

In theory, Friday in the Islamic world is a quieter time—equivalent to our Sunday. On Friday, I try to sleep late to restore my reserves. As mentioned in the prior *Kurier*, I try to get "drunk" with sleep. In the morning, I make a stiff cup of instant Kava coffee crusted with creamer and sweetener, ½ artificial and ½ natural sugar made with my little electric water pot that in a quick minute steams fiercely and merrily away. I then lie down in my little bed with my laptop balanced across my pulled-up knees and write this *Kurier* for an hour or two. To my left—keeping watch over me—are two watercolors I acquired from local artists to add a splash of color to my room. One is a wizened Pashtun "graybeard" tribesman and former fighter tenderly holding an infant; the other is a painting of a fully veiled Afghan woman peering out from under her hijab with extraordinarily beautiful blue-green-gold eyes of the type they find in remote and dangerous Nuristan.

Because I don't want to interrupt my focus, I will have loaded up on breakfast stuff—cereal, power bars, an apple—the night before so I don't have to emerge from my room until later in the morning. Finally, the coffee will drive me out to our generally clean public bathroom. I've noticed that national habits occasionally kick in, most tellingly in bathrooms. While most occupants are neat, some fastidiously so, a few others are not or simply do not know better. And then there are others who, by custom or religion, wash their feet in the public drain or—as I discovered quite by accident—in the sink where we all brush our teeth.

After living close-in like this for months on end, other little habits and idiosyncrasies develop. One is the rush in early morning for the shower with the best spigot and a ledge next to the window for your towel. I'm convinced that some get up earlier just to get this superior stall. At night I am usually the last to enter the billeting area. From under the doors, I can hear the Babel of numerous voices and tongues in their rooms chattering away all over the world on Skype. Although very slow and erratic, we do have Internet in our rooms. If it's not hopelessly late, I often join in too. Finally, it's usually way too late when I turn off my light. Close to midnight, I often read a few pages of a book or magazine then scribe a diary page after saying my prayers. By the time I departed ISAF in early January for my Norfolk course, I had already amassed over 200 days of diary entries.

On occasional Fridays, I check the situation across the region and then amble out to one of the two bazaars, either at ISAF or Camp Eggers. These well-stocked and chaotic on-base bazaars are a big deal for Afghan merchants. ISAF troops stopped going out into Kabul and to bustling "Chicken Street" almost three years ago for force protection reasons. All merchants—from 10-year-old hucksters to crafty 60-year-old traders—hail us with "My Friend, my friend," even if we're meeting for the first time.

A trip to the bazaar is pretty much the only dependable diversion to take our minds off the fray and stress for a moment. For those of us sequestered most of the time in our bases, it is easy to forget that well into 2004, ISAF troops could freely walk and visit within Kabul. Because we can no longer walk about the city openly, we must seem all the more distant and foreign to the local Kabuli population.

During my assignment, I have accumulated distinctive Afghan items, including colorful tribal garb, handicrafts, and carpets that I send home for Christmas. Gems, especially emeralds, rubies, and star sapphires, are also bountiful, but buyer beware! As a history buff, I also got drawn to the wide range of Afghans' historic firearms. Many were left behind by invaders and occupiers after being defeated, ejected, or worse, massacred. I confess that I've been able to pick up nice Enfield, Tower, Snider percussion muskets, and an Imperial (not East India Company) Brown Bess, that possibly may have been at the Battle of Gandamak in 1842. I also found one of those iconic British Victorian-era Martini-Henry rifles. This first pure breech-loader conceivably could have been picked up by some victorious Pathan after the crushing British defeat at Maiwand, near Kandahar, in 1880. It also was the Martini-Henry rifle that Michael Caine and his redcoats hefted in that 1964 glory-filled epic movie *Zulu*. Finally, I have an excellent example of a slender, well-decorated, and embossed 1800s-era Afghan Jezail—a lethal long-range shooter in the hands of a good marksman, which the Afghans invariably were and still are.

OUT AND ABOUT IN KABUL

WHEN I CAN, I BRIEFLY foray out of our ISAF compound to visit various security chiefs, the Afghan National Army (ANA), the Ministry of Interior, the National Directorate of Security (NDS), and the Kabul Police. After polite choreography and always over tea, raisins, and pistachios, these meetings are interesting discussions with hardened individuals, who all have lived, participated in, and survived the dreadful battering of Afghanistan that has been ongoing since 1978.

Some of the people I met were former Mujahideen who had fought the Soviets in the 1980s. Several were former communist Afghan Army officers, and all were in one group or another during the gruesome Civil War (1992–1996) that wrecked Afghanistan even more than the Soviets. They were also all Muslims, representing various levels of piety, who fought the extremism of the al-Qaeda-backed Taliban before and after 9/11. While talking eye-to-eye with them, I often wonder what goes on in their minds and the horrors they and their families have seen.

Some of my visits across town are not in full military garb, enabling me to move more subtly around Kabul's bustling, traffic-filled streets and in and out of meetings. We can pass as UN or NGO workers without closely shorn hair and rarely get a second glance, especially if traveling discreetly with scarves on in a non-nondescript SUV instead of moving by convoy. Our holstered pistols are discreetly worn behind our hip, covered by a jacket, and our protective vests are often covered as well. This is particularly useful because we look less menacing to the locals, especially children. We want to appear in full battle regalia at other times, but not in downtown Kabul on a non-locked-down day.

I make this point about casual garb and mixing in because one of the critical requirements of successful counterinsurgencies is showing a steady and secure presence while working on the essential separation of the insurgents from the population. Suppose we are not regularly out and among the Afghans and are seen mostly driving by in closed-off-armored convoys (even if for justifiable security reasons)—we become more foreign and alien to the teeming population just outside our gates.

After one office call, we impulsively stopped at Kabul's lightly visited and walled Babur's Garden. This tranquil green tree-endowed spot is one of the only places in the city where one can go and feel time slow down and sense a bit of normalcy. Families were picnicking, and unchaperoned young lovers, typically split apart, edged closer to one another than on more public Kabul streets. One Tajik family group asked to have their pictures taken with us. I heard children laughing, the joyful sound of playgrounds. My God, what a wonderful sound that is, especially when deprived of such for months.

Babur, the founder of the great Moghul Empire, created this twenty-seven-acre, walled plot of secluded land. He became so enamored of this idyllic spot that his body was brought from India and buried in the Garden after his death in 1530. His small gravestone, humble for a ruler so great, is made of black and rose marble and was placed next to a small mosque that today bears the scars of the 1990s Civil War. During these fierce "Mujahideen Nights," when Ahmad Shah Massoud fought Gulbuddin Hekmatyar, and both fought the Hazaras, the summer palace was ravaged. All the trees on the property were chopped down for firewood. Renovated in 2002 with funding from the Agha Khan, this Garden is one of the few places where one can slow down, think, take stock, and regain perspective away from the incessant buzz of an active headquarters and the frenetic din and hubbub of a chaotic and overcrowded city.

UP OVER THE EASTERN HINTERLAND - GARDEZ AND GHAZNI

AFTER MY INITIAL SEVERAL-MONTH-LONG KABUL "baptism by fire," I started to get out more across diverse Afghanistan to visit the many elements—the U.S., Allied, and Afghan—that are conducting the critical rural and urban work essential for success in this counterinsurgency.

I was able to get out to all the major Regional Commands (RCs) in the East, South, West, and North and Center in Kabul—no easy thing to accomplish, thanks to the erratic nature of securing timely multi-national airlift around the theatre. Several times I have been delayed in "Strandahar" (a nickname for Kandahar) due to airlift burdens. The bulk of my visits have focused on the American-heavy RC East, the hub of which is the vast Bagram Airbase which is about a 70-minute drive from ISAF Headquarters in Kabul. (I flew into this airbase in June 2008, when my assignment began.)

The insurgencies in the East are quite different in complexion than in RC South. I use the plural "insurgencies" because several significant groups are involved within the eastern zone for distinct reasons. We use the term "syndicate" to describe this opportunistic medley of groups, including Haqqani and Hekmatyar, with pedigrees going back to the anti-Soviet struggle of the 1980s.

On one such outing, we flew by Blackhawk helicopter to see the Khost-Gardez (KG) Pass over which a crucial paved road is being built to better connect important and geographically isolated Khost Province with the rest of Afghanistan. Khost Province, in the southeast, is essentially a lowland bowl that protrudes into Pakistan and is girdled by hills to its rear. During the Soviet occupation, the Mujahideen were able to isolate Khost by occupying the hills, including the KG Pass area that connects it to the rest of Afghanistan. They fought to prevent the Russians from keeping the road open. A good account of the Mujahideen's strategy can be found in *The Bear Trap*, written by a former Pakistani ISI (Inter-Service Intelligence) officer. The road currently being built is to preclude a successful repeat of this insurgent strategy from the 1980s. Below us, we could see various trucks and commerce laboring up past pockets of well-guarded road construction rigs ascending this sinuous road over

84

the tawny, timber-denuded landscape—more than one hundred kilometers long. The U.S. outpost that overwatches this area is appropriately named Forward Operating Base (FOB) Wilderness. Last summer and early autumn the base was being rocketed and mortared almost every night. A number of the senior insurgents prosecuting attacks against us here and elsewhere are the same men that fought the Soviets *with our support* twenty years ago. Bottom line: the terrain, and therefore most tactics, stays the same, regardless of the cast of characters.

On another short helicopter foray, I was able to see the strategic Highway 1 between Kabul and Ghazni from the air. This high-volume stretch of the Ring Road connecting Kabul to Kandahar and up to Herat was completed with major fanfare and optimism in 2003. Interestingly, strategic roads in congested areas always seem to be "Highway 1." (See Bernard Fall's *Street Without Joy,* about 1950s Indochina, one of the best books about counter-insurgency ever written.) The Taliban and other insurgents, increasingly, and especially last summer, targeted this road and commerce to disrupt coalition and Afghan freedom of movement, a move designed to increase Afghan paranoia that the cities, particularly Kabul, were being isolated.

As we flew over the long, mostly straight road, all appeared normal in stretches until when we could see clusters of burnt-out, bell-laden "jingle trucks" or scorched areas of highway where trucks and commerce had been destroyed and left to melt into the hot tarmac. The color along this stretch was monotonously beige, occasionally punctuated with patches of luxurious, verdant green where irrigation and a better water table allowed crops to be grown adjacent to the many villages along the road.

After a difficult couple of months, aggressive operations by the coalition and Afghans mostly regained this key road. I saw several long Afghan commercial convoys from the air escorted by gun-toting HUMVEEs and the new, heavily armored MRAPs (Mine Resistant Ambush Protected) that—thanks to their heavy armor and high, angled undercarriage—provide our troops with much-improved protection from the ever-present IEDs.

On this little foray, we alighted inside the important and active Provincial Reconstruction Team (PRT) in Ghazni, a key location on the Kabul-Kandahar trade route that skirts the Hindu Kush to the south. The twenty-six PRTs across the country are the primary day-to-day "soft power" transmitters of assistance and presence on behalf of the ISAF and allied nations. The insurgents frequently target them because the enemy understands these elements link daily with the local population over which the current struggle for security, hearts, and minds is fought.

Ghazni, formerly a well-visited tourist site up into the 1970s, thrived in a Buddhist incarnation and later under the Muslims. Its high-water mark was its time as the center of Mahmoud the Great's Ghaznavid Empire. Ghazni's golden age was abruptly extinguished in a ghastly day or two by the Mongols in 1221. Some distinctive structures remain, including the Palace and Mausoleum of Mahmoud and some weathered minarets. Today, this small Afghan city is known for its carpets. I was able to obtain a lovely rough little hand-woven golden Ghazni runner, the charm of which was its handmade tones in natural vegetable dyes. Ghazni today is being patrolled by a proud Polish contingent. They have been with us through thick and thin since the fall of the Berlin Wall in 1989 and continue to serve here quite capably in often difficult circumstances.

The strategic Ring Road in terrain-constrained Afghanistan is critical for moving within its provinces. It girdles the entire nation and links the four main cities. The roads within the mountainous central region are basically dirt, weather-dependent, and snake their way across and through some of the roughest terrain in the world.

Besides being critical for coalition movement and supplies, freedom of safe movement along roads is a barometer of perceived Afghan security. Until 2006 an Afghan family could travel with a high assurance of safety to visit relatives along the Ring Road from Kabul to either Kandahar or Mazar and then to Herat. While today's situation is better than the brutal summer/fall of 2008, only Kabul to Mazar is relatively safe for civilian traffic. However, commerce out of necessity flows across all the arteries.

Persian Legacy - Herat

As the JIOC-A Director and as of October 1st, the newly appointed U.S. Forces-Afghanistan (USFOR-A) J2 senior intelligence officer until March 2009, I travel periodically to locations where both U.S. and NATO/ISAF forces are conducting missions together. These trips are often far from Kabul and U.S.-centric Bagram. For example, I visited Herat in the far West, where some U.S. military are deployed in the Afghan Regional Security Integration Command (ARSIC)-West. For centuries, this historic city was the easternmost and wealthy outpost of Persia and the Safavid Empire. Today, Herat remains well within the Iranian sphere of interest.

We landed in an old twin-engined German C-160 Transall at Herat airbase. As soon as I looked around, I could easily detect the Persian influence in the architecture and the fact that Herat had the best road network in Afghanistan, second only to the roads around Mazar in the North. Relative prosperity was on full display here, which I must emphasize is largely due to significant Iranian investment in the region. So, while we view dimly some of Iran's more "greyarea" arms and drug precursor smuggling activities in Afghanistan, Iranians do also provide a vital measure of economic stability to the region.

To the south toward Farah, we see a growing insurgency, as well as to the North in Badghis Province, both of which are vital connector points for the nationwide ring road, as I mentioned earlier. A typical Afghan family simply cannot travel safely anymore, a hard fact that only adds to the population's current high sense of security unease.

There is one other alternative, but it's seasonal: a route directly west along bumpy, unpaved roads across the mountainous west of Afghanistan. This "improved" dirt road is essentially shut down during winter, so it's useful only during good weather. That leaves only the Ring Road to transit goods along the ground between Afghanistan's main four cities, Kabul, Kandahar, Herat, and Mazar. This cross-country route passes through remote Chagcharan, where a Lithuanian Provincial Reconstruction Team (PRT) sits as ISAF's deepest outpost. (For insight into this route, see Rory Stewart's engaging and uplifting *The Places in Between*.) Unfortunately, even this road, which enters impoverished Ghowr Province from the west, is also not completely safe anymore. Even adventurous souls like Stewart would now have an incredibly challenging time visiting the remote 12th-century Minaret at Jam that, based on photos I've seen, is surely at least a runner-up for one of the Wonders of the Medieval world. The reasons why such an amazing structure was erected in the most remote area of Afghanistan—far from any civilization centers—are lost to time. Pushing further across this rugged area, one can enter Bamian and come face to face with the remnants of gigantic twin Buddhas so tragically defaced at the hands of the Taliban. Visiting Bamian and Jam are my two cultural "Holy Grails" of this deployment.

After conducting business at the Italian/Spanish NATO base (Camp Arena), we visited the U.S. element at the Afghan Regional Security Command - West (ARSIC-W) at nearby Camp Stone. A key point to emphasize is that U.S. forces "in harm's way" are located in the East and South and at lower densities within the more Allied west and north. Part of CSTC-A (Combined Security Transition Command-Afghanistan), they work hard to develop the Afghan National Army and Police into coherent fighting and security forces, the success of which is our coalition ticket out of

Afghanistan. This will take time, but great strides have been made. Already Afghans are leading many operations with our brave ETT (Embedded Tactical Training) and PMTs (Police Mentor Teams) in close attendance.

While in the area, I was able to spend a few hours inside bustling Herat. The jewel of the city is the so-called Friday Mosque built in 1200 CE. This beautifully preserved structure sits in the very center of the city. Its distinctive oriental blue dome stands out gorgeously from any direction, especially when spotlighted in the early morning and late afternoon by the ever-present sun.

We then drove by the jagged remnants of seven Minarets at Musalla that, even in their blasted, eroded state, hint at the awesomeness of what they must have looked like during the height of the post-Mongol Timurid Renaissance. When you get close to these broken minarets, all standing crookedly and lonely in various states of disrepair, surrounded by fallow fields, it is impossible not to be awed by their grandeur and height. In 1937, Robert Byron wrote after visiting the complex: "Strolling up the road towards the minarets, I feel as one might who has lighted on the lost books of Livy or an unknown Botticelli. It is impossible, I suppose, to communicate such a feeling." (From Christina Lamb's *The Sewing*

Circles of Herat, from which I will quote heavily). Considering that they are all that is left of the original twenty-one minarets, one can only imagine how this incredible madrasa complex and mausoleum must have looked in their heyday.

The minarets at Musalla have been silent witnesses to the ebb and flow of would-be or actual conquerors of Afghanistan. While the extensive building complex crumbled under these ravages, the great minarets survived Uzbek and Persian plunder and fell in 1749 under the rule of the first great Pashtun king, Ahmad Shah Abdali. Many assign blame for the final destruction of this complex to the Soviets. However, during the so-called "Great Game" between Russia and England in the 1880s, the British tore down what remained of the complex to prevent Russia from using it as cover during an anticipated attack. The attack never came. But by then, it was too late to save the buildings.

Byron commented on the British decision:

"The most glorious productions of Mohammedan architecture in the XVth century, having survived the barbarism of four centuries were now razed to the ground under the eyes and with the approval of the English Commissioners."

At the time of our visit, the only building remaining in this complex was a tomb inside the mausoleum of Gawhar Shad Begum ("Happy Pearl"), daughter-in-law of the dreaded Mongol conqueror Tamerlane. She was a princess of Mongol and Turkic descent with an extraordinarily strong personality and is one of just a handful of women to leave an indelible impression on Islamic history. Chroniclers of this turbulent era called her the Bilquis (Queen of Sheba) of her time, a sentiment inscribed on her tombstone within the mausoleum.

Gawhar brings to mind another strong female character in Afghanistan history: Malalai, who in 1880, as the legend goes, died with Royal Afghan forces at Maiwand during a battle with the British. While most Western historiographies focus on the heroic last stand of the 66th Berkshire regiment at Maiwand and "Bobbie," the regiment's little dog mascot, the story of Malalai is equally compelling. While on the battlefield tending to the Afghan wounded, she saw the Afghan ranks wavering and strode to the front line calling out and shaming the mostly Pashtun men:

"Young love! If you do not fall in the battle of Maiwand, By God, someone is saving you as a symbol of shame!

Chastened by her call to their pride and vanity, the Afghan fighters and ghazis strengthened, and the line held. At that moment, a flag bearer fell, and Malalai ran forward and picked it up. While waving it, she further encouraged the men by singing a Landai (a Pashtun woman's verse) before she fell to a British Martini-Henry bullet. Her last words were:

"With a drop of my sweetheart's blood, Shed in defense of the Motherland, Will I put a beauty spot on my forehead?"

Maiwand was a disastrous British defeat. Coming on the heels of the ferocious Zulu massacre of the 24th Regiment (South Wales Borderers) at Isandlwana the year before, Maiwand represented the nadir of Victorian British arms.

Today, many Pashtun girls are named Malalai. Both the revered stories of Gawhar Shah and Malalai reveal a disconnect between Afghan legend and the harsh reality of women living in rural Afghanistan today. One hopes that the reality and not just the mythology of women in Afghanistan improves over time, especially outside the cities.

The beautiful city of Herat was the earliest victim of the Soviet invasion. In late 1979, several warlords led by a former Afghan Army officer, Ismail Khan, rose collectively in a savage reaction to the heavy-handed Soviet occupation—the first indicator to the Soviets that their invasion of Afghanistan was going to be both problematic and bloody. In the ensuing fighting, much of Herat was bombed into submission.

Sixteen years later, the Taliban also had a challenging time subduing Herat's more moderate egalitarian spirit after they conquered it in 1995. Within Herat, always considered Afghanistan's most progressive city, passive resistance to the Taliban manifested in many ways that showed the more refined urban populace's scorn and contempt for the leaders who had shut down music, forced beard growth, and forbade girls from girls attending schools. According to Christina Lamb, insouciant Herati kids would sneak up behind the stick or whip-wielding Taliban moral police and then recite the last two lines in Dari of the poem below and run away.

I told you to say your beard is long And under it are the plans of a Saudi
You moral policeman in the middle of a bazaar are as greedy as a long tailed
donkey in a trough

Of Mullah Omar taking the sacred Cloak of the Prophet Mohammed from its shrine in Kandahar and declaring himself Amir-ul Momineem" (Commander of the Faithful) the Herati poet Khafash wrote "Congratulations for cloaking a pile of dung with an asses skin."

While Herat has many issues, including dangerous insurgent activity to the south in Farah and the north in Badghis, it remains a center of relative stability compared to Kandahar and the troublesome south. Its biggest security problem is major organized crime. A modern-day Golem named Gholam Yahya, an opportunistic local criminal who masks himself as an insurgent, has persistently created problems for the coalition in the area.

NORTH OF THE HINDU KUSH

IN MID-NOVEMBER, I BROKE AWAY from ISAF HQ in Kabul for a four-day site assistance visit to the North, the one area in Afghanistan where convoys can drive on excellent roads with relatively minimal risk of being attacked (if one drives prudently.) Winter, which starts early in Northern Afghanistan, was approaching, so we pushed hard to depart before snow in the highlands made this trip problematic.

We embarked in a small convoy of up-armored Land Cruisers that coupled speed, ruggedness, and relative discretion in a country whose roads are full of SUVs belonging to ISAF, NGOs, UN, the Afghan government, warlords, power brokers, and crime lords. They are infinitely more discreet than HUMVEEs and impossible for an attacker to identify as an ISAF coalition at night until we are safely past them. This is the key with those insurgents or criminals waiting with IEDs or small arms—make them hesitate before firing or launching and get past them before they have time to reconsider.

We drove over 1200 kilometers from the sprawling Bagram Airbase north through the Shomali Plain, an area devastated by Soviet Hind helicopter attacks trying to repel regular Mujahideen attacks against the airbase. The Salang Tunnel was the essential lifeline to Afghanistan's capital and East. Even today, one can see the remnants of buildings and compounds pulverized by the Russians to keep the pesky Afghan fighters away from Bagram.

THE PANJSHIR VALLEY - HEART OF THE RESISTANCE

As we approached the highlands to the North, we turned northeast into the "Lion's Gate," the gateway to the Panjshir Valley, representing the heart of the resistance against the Soviets and, later, the Taliban. Dominated by the Panjshiris (who are nicknamed "Tajiks on steroids"), this sinuous, gorgeous valley has been a thorn in the side of all invaders who want access to the all-important Highway. Ahmed Shah Massoud's fighters launched raids and attacks against the Soviets and the Taliban from this stronghold. The Soviets launched multiple offensives into the Panjshir, with formidable armor, mechanized and later, heliborne forces, but never could take this key terrain. Even today, Soviet equipment litters the Valley. One can trace their progress, or lack thereof, by observing the numerous stripped-down faded green hulks of mostly T-62s, BMPs, BTRs, and BRDMs strewn across the valley landscape.

The entryway into the Valley is akin to a wine bottle's cork—narrow and a proper funnel. Our military-trained eyes immediately noted that it would be impossible for major forces to enter the valley on a broad front. The well-kept two-lane road was flanked by the rapidly flowing Panjshir River, limiting an invader to a front no wider than about 100 yards for the first few miles into the valley—a less than ideal beginning to any campaign.

I love water, so seeing the fast-flowing bottle-green mountain torrent cut through tall, formidable granite walls was pure pleasure after almost a half year of driving past and over the mostly dried up Kabul River. After several miles, the landscape gradually widened to reveal a latticework of little villages, compounds, and well irrigated, cultivated fields. Rice and vegetables were grown in carefully terraced layers. Up here is an American PRT that, while remote, must be the most desirable stationing location in all of Afghanistan. In terms of security and friendly population, it would be tough to find a better berth.

While seemingly relaxed while going on about their business, the villagers are watchful and are quick to detect strangers in their midst. About halfway up the Valley, we could see the gold painted dome of Ahmad Shah Massoud's tomb. It is sited high on the mountainside, offering a wonderful panorama to both the northeast and southwest. At the time of our visit, the tomb was being transformed into an entire shrine and visitors' center. It was here that Massoud was killed on September 9, 2001, just two days before the 9/11 attacks on the World Trade Center and Pentagon, by an al-Qaeda suicide operative posing as a French journalist with a camera bomb.

The Panjshir Valley reminded me of the equally beautiful but smaller Rugova Valley that snakes from Western Kosovo near Pec into Albania. Besides its sheer beauty and symbol of resistance, the Panjshir is home to stunning gems, including emeralds that are mined in the Valley's uplands. For an enjoyable read about the Afghan gem trade, see Gary Bowersox's *The Gem Hunter.*

It is essential to dwell on the Panjshir Valley a bit because if there is any one place in Afghanistan that signifies determined and implacable resistance, it is there. These proud and formidable mountain warriors—"Tajiks on steroids—proved to be unconquerable by the vastly more powerful Soviets and, ten years later, by the more numerous Pashtun Taliban. Today, they are more or less allies of our coalition. The Panjshir is one of the few places in Afghanistan where we can truly move around with absolute certainty that an ambush or IED will not be waiting for us around some road curve or under a culvert. So proud are the Panjshiris of their landscape and the hospitality and protection they offer therein; they are a bit offended if we move around within their area in our customary helmets and flak jackets.

Through the Salang Tunnel

From the Panjshir Valley, we drove a short distance back to Highway 1 and then headed north, ascending through numerous galleries and switch-back roads to the strategic Salang Tunnel. Reaching an elevation of more than 11,000 feet, this road and tunnel are an engineering feat for which the Soviets can take ample credit. Built in the 1960s, it connected Kabul to the North and the Soviet Union. Without this road and tunnel, vehicular access to the North was limited to the crude Ring Road.

Traversing this switch-backed stretch of road was one of the most incredible visual treats I have ever enjoyed, matching a ride I took over the Georgian Military Highway and past Caucasus peaks in 1991 during the last months of the USSR. (Read Ralph Peters' _Looking for Trouble_ for a detailed account of this adventure.) We passed pastoral scenes and activities that probably have not changed much from a thousand years ago. At the lower elevations, we saw

Kuchi goat herders and dogs tending their flocks. This activity often appeared to be family affairs, but one also spotted solo young boys carrying staffs and escorting the four-footed source of their family's wealth. Also, trodding along these traditional routes were overladen, horse-driven carts and small trucks with entire families bundled up atop them. We even encountered several strings of Bactrian camels plodding their way along the road, looking just like their counterparts from a millennia ago, except for the wares they were hauling.

Upon entering the tunnel, it was instantly evident that the Salang is an engineering feat, albeit crudely hewn. Inside, the soot-blackened walls lacked the rounded curves, softened edges, or tiled surfaces one would see in a lowlands western tunnel. The interior was claustrophobically dark and clouded with an opaque veil of vehicle exhaust and dust that our headlights strained to penetrate. Overburdened blowers worked hard to keep the air inside breathable.

We were not alone. Afghan commerce included ubiquitous wheezing and diesel-spewing "jingle trucks" that crawled along inside the tunnel, navigating the darkness with barely visible running lights. As we made our way through the tunnel, we remarked among ourselves that there were bound to be ghosts and zombies. An estimated 178 Soviet troops and eight hundred Afghans suffocated or burned to death on November 3, 1982, when a vehicle accident involving a Soviet military convoy led to a fire inside the Salang. The tragedy earned the dubious honor of being the worse road accident in global history.

After making our way for 1.6 miles through this amazing tube under the Hindu Kush "Continental Divide," we emerged into the fresh, clean air of highland Northern Afghanistan with great relief. All around us were glorious, snow-capped mountains of the Hindu Kush. The air temperature immediately dipped more than 10–20 degrees Fahrenheit. We descended into a dense cloud bank and precipitation that socked us in for the duration of our journey up north. Our heavily ladened Land Cruiser negotiated the slick road like a champ. At the same time, many Afghan vehicles pulled aside to put on chains; some bought from enterprising Tajiks who somehow got their wares and chains for sale up to little shacks near the pass's summit.

Trucks ground their way downhill carefully in first gear, fearful of sliding off the road and plunging into the dark abyss. Seeing all this made me imagine how difficult and challenging it must have been for the Soviets to regularly cross this pass with large military convoys harried by ambushes on both sides in the lower elevations.

Upon reaching level ground, we entered the vast steppe and

desert that is Northern Central Asia. On roads that matched some in quality within Western Europe, we passed the District Center of Pol e Khumri site and into the southern portion of the "Baglan Pocket," one of the Pashtun insurgency hot spots in the north. Two U.S. soldiers were killed by a suicide bomber just two weeks before our arrival while visiting an Afghan police headquarters. All that was left of the likely young Pakistani Pashtun suicide bomber was a pathetically scruffy shock of disheveled hair that looked more like a dirty mop than a head. Two solitary legs were also found blown off below the knees, still in tattered Afghan Police garb. I wondered how the mythical 72 Virgins of Paradise would receive the mangled remnants of the Muslim youth who had dreamed of martyrdom.

While the north is by far the safest place to move in Afghanistan, there are several Pashtun populated pockets where the Taliban never completely departed after being thrown from power in 2001. They create problems for some of the coalition soldiers—notably German, Swedish, and Hungarian—who must adhere to strict rules. The Norwegians in the northwest in Maymaneh are permitted to be far more aggressive. While in the Baglan Corridor, we visited the Hungarian PRT in Pole Khumri and the German PRT in Kunduz, which was the Northern capital of the Taliban until being ejected in

2001. We encountered hostile looks and glares only on this stretch of road, including the rantings of what appeared to be the town fool as we fueled up with gas from a public station. Everywhere else in the north, we received waves and "thumbs-ups" from the population—especially kids—as well as an occasional subtle and discreet wave from a burqa clad woman.

I was struck by how cold everybody appeared in the North. Most work is done outdoors. Much of the rural commercial activity is roadside, and most of the overwhelmingly male working population was outside working in unheated shacks and stalls. Clad in sandals, Afghan men huddled and hunched, stamping their cold feet around fires, and slouched along the roadside wrapped in their distinctive brown, black, or dung-colored blanket shawls worn all year long. As is their habit, some men kept a corner of their headscarf between their teeth to help hold it in place. Others wore longer, quilted green and blue Karzai jackets. We saw many children with book packs walking back and forth to school, including—most encouragingly— white-scarved girls of all ages. Though the public arena is still male-dominant, we could see plenty of burqaed women, some wearing white, most clad in blue shrouds.

As Afghan men probably do, I started to look at the wrists and feet of these women, many of whom wore modern, stylish shoes and bracelets that were one way an Afghan woman could subtly display self-expression. I'm told that some women actually prefer the relative solitude and cocoon that wearing an anonymous burqa provides against male leering and touching. That is just another perspective on a style of dress that makes many of us in the West recoil against the most traditional aspects of Afghan society.

In Mazar, we visited the German Headquarters at Camp Marmal to talk with their senior intelligence officer, a very situationally aware Swede. We then moved on to ARSIC-North, where the U.S. trains and mentors the Afghan Army and Police, unbeknownst to many. (Each region has a U.S. program for such training efforts.)

While providing training and mentoring, American soldiers work side-by-side with Afghan Army units in their fight against insurgents. Several have died supporting the Afghans in this critical confidence and capacity-building mission. This training and mentoring effort, assisted by the U.S. and Allied OMLTs (Operational Mentor and Liaison Team), is key to our collective long-term success in Afghanistan. In essence, the training effort represents the "Afghanistanization " of the complex security effort in Afghanistan.

In the end, one day, we will be gone, and the Afghans will have to shoulder the brunt of their security challenges. We also visited the OMLT in Mazar, a facility heavily staffed by a very capable Finnish contingent.

During this period, the main focus of our attention was the country-wide strategic effort to ensure a widely represented and credible voter registration process in anticipation of August's presidential elections. In the north, the mixed and primarily Tajik, Uzbek, and Turkmen populations, including women, signed up in large numbers in the hope they could challenge the Pashtun lock on the presidency, currently occupied by Hamid Karzai.

While in Mazar, we took the mandatory short drive to the dun-colored walls of ancient Balkh. Two thousand years ago, the city was the pre-eminent center for commerce along the famed Silk Road. Cold winds gusted from the Northern Steppes, slicing us to the bone as we stood atop Balkh's battered parapets pondering the vibrant civilization that once stood here on this key trade route. It was Alexander the Great who made Balkh famous by dwelling here for almost three years and marrying Roxana, the Bactrian "luminous beauty."

Balkh thrived for centuries, surviving the ebb and flow of conquerors and empires until being destroyed en masse by the ruthless, rampaging Mongols in 1221. Marco Polo wrote of his

111

visit there just fifty years after that horrific moment. Within the site's broken walls, we were able to dig out some of the distinctive teal blue glazed ceramic that covered walls and cupolas of later Balkh (and much of the Islamic world). Today, one must use vivid imagination to transform today's faded walls of current Balkh—with the notable exception of eye-catching Masjid Sabz (Green) Mosque—into an image of a thriving, influential metropolis. I'm reminded of that well-known sonnet about Ozymandias by poet Percy Bysshe Shelley:

I met a traveller from an antique land,

Who said— "Two vast and trunkless legs of stone

Stand in the desert.... Near them, on the sand,

Half sunk a shattered visage lies, whose frown,

And wrinkled lip, and sneer of cold command,

Tell that its sculptor well those passions read

Which yet survive, stamped on these lifeless things,

The hand that mocked them, and the heart that fed.

And on the pedestal, these words appear:

My name is Ozymandias, King of Kings.

Look on my Works, ye Mighty, and despair!

Nothing beside remains. Round the decay

Of that colossal Wreck, boundless and bare
The lone and level sands stretch far away.".

Upon departing the German Headquarters, we made sure to stop by Mazar's Blue Mosque. All major roads in Mazar funnel into a circle over which this extraordinarily beautiful structure looms. And it is indeed blue—that lovely crenulated teal-blue shade that adorns the walls and domes of much of Central Asian Islamic architecture. While visiting, we passed lines of beggars—a symbol of the decline of a proud warrior society. Many possessed only one limb, a reminder of the massive number of mines that the Soviets, the Communist Afghan Army, and later various warring Mujahideen factions indiscriminately sowed across the landscape. It is particularly wrenching to see teenaged youth—both boys and girls—with single limbs, the sad result of herding in fields not entirely cleared by robust demining efforts.

There was a lively hubbub around the mosque; the crowd included many burqaed women. I stood close to the walls and touched its smooth, blue-tiled surface, marveling at the superb craftsmanship that even today's artisans might have difficulty matching. As non-Muslims, we could not enter the inner sanctum of the Mosque,

113

though most who saw us were friendly. I took great effort, as always do, to cross my right hand over my heart, bow slightly, and say "As-Salaam-Alaikum," e.g., "May peace be upon you," which almost invariably engenders a similar response and softens any anti-foreigner sentiment the local may harbor.

THE CONTESTED SOUTH - KANDAHAR AND LASHKAR GAH

AFTER OUR WHIRLWIND VISIT TO so many places new to me, I returned to Kandahar, where I have a detachment of about thirty-five personnel. It is here in Kandahar that the Taliban movement was born. The insurgents in this area have heavily stressed the undermanned Canadian, British, Dutch, Australian, and increasingly U.S. contingents that comprise most of RC South's bulk.

It is important to keep in mind that this mostly Pashtun insurgency is found in the religiously conservative and culturally backward countryside. The most conservative countryside in all of Afghanistan is the Pashtun south, followed by the southeast and northeast. This conservative demographic does not necessarily fit well within the more inclusive, multi-ethnic, and—by Afghan standards—more open-minded cities such as Kabul, Herat, or Mazar.

Complex Kandahar is another story, however. When you hear

of the stalemated struggle in Afghanistan's south, it will be this arid Southern region (including Helmand, Uruzgan, and Zabul provinces) where we face our greatest challenges. (But that doesn't mean there isn't plenty of action underway elsewhere, particularly in the East and West.) This southern region is the heart of the Pashtun-dominated insurgency and where major coalition efforts are underway to reverse the tenuous situation there.

While visiting the many units in the Kandahar area, I was itching to get out to the military locations outside of the area, particularly Lashkar Gah, which I think will get considerably more attention in the years ahead. Lashkar, located on the fertile Helmand River Valley, sits astride the heart of Afghanistan's notorious Poppy Belt.

It's worth looking at a map of this area. Most maps mark it as a pure desert, but the Helmand River valley provides life-giving sustenance to over 1.5 million people. This area was a major American development in the 1960s. Few know that Lashkar was a USAID planned agricultural community, and apparently, there are residual tendrils of goodwill toward the U.S. left among the elders. The problem is that much of this fertile area transitioned to lucrative poppy cultivation, replacing foodstuffs. Two suburbs of Lashkar— Nad Ali and Marjah—are aggressively contested by the insurgents and are among the largest poppy-growing areas in Afghanistan and, therefore, the world.

For an interesting little read about the poppy challenge in the south, pick up Joel Hafvenstein's easily absorbed *Opium Season,* about his dangerous year (2004–2005) in Lashkar working for an NGO and trying to establish alternative livelihoods to growing poppy.

One bright morning, we flew to Lashkar in two olive drab Royal Navy Commando Sea Stallion helicopters that roared at high-speed over the inhospitable desert from Kandahar. As a kid, I always admired British military aviation; their aircraft was marked distinctively with blue- and burgundy-colored roundels. As we flew, door gunners craned their necks out the side doors. The ungainly "birds" zigzagged their way between dunes and rocky outcrops and then descended rapidly into the British base that headquarters Task Force Helmand. We received detailed briefs on the complex micro-campaign ongoing against the Taliban and associated criminals seldom reported by the press.

That night, under cover of darkness, we boarded a powerful British CH-47 Chinook of the type that was first fielded during Vietnam and has been upgraded numerous times since then. Despite its distinctly un-aerodynamic look, this blacked-out, twin-rotor workhouse is still the fastest helicopter in our inventory. After a quick take-off, we turned east, gaining altitude over the safer eastern districts before turning west and flying west high over contested Nad Ali to Camp Bastion, a large logistics base and airfield in Western Helmand Province. No fewer than four times, we were startled by shockingly bright, sensitively set anti-missile flares that fired on us from stubby pylons. You will read much of Kandahar and Helmand in the years ahead.

Returning to the Home Front

ALMOST SEVEN MONTHS PASSED IN Afghanistan before I returned to Germany for my mid-tour leave. It was quite an interesting flight. I was dozing in a seat behind the C-17 cockpit when I was jolted awake at about 3 a.m. by a big thump. A few minutes later we thumped again, so I peeked into the cockpit and was somewhat startled to see in the star-lit ambient darkness, not more than 20 yards in front and 20 yards above us, the big, well-lit tail end of a KC-135 tanker, with fuel nozzle extended, fueling our massive transport aircraft. The pilots held the giant aircraft steady while positioning the plane's head and fuel aperture to line up with the tanker's fuel boom and nozzle. All the while, a bank of multi-color lights blinked red-amber-green to signal the state of alignment. This delicate process went on for over forty minutes and once again reinforced to me that projection of power does not necessarily mean combat systems, but rather, the ability to somewhere over Central Asia, Turkey, the Arabian

Sea, or anywhere else in the world, mate up two massive aircraft to refuel mid-air. Even more impressive, our Air Force pilots do these operations dozens of times a day and make a very complex and dangerous task look amazingly routine.

We finally landed in Ramstein, Germany, and I happily slumped—without body armor, helmet, and pistol—into the plush back seat of a fast Audi sedan. During the hour-long drive to Heidelberg, I marveled at the trees and how lush and green the landscape was. The roads and autobahns were stocked with sleek, fast machines and were orderly, well-lit, and uniformly marvelous—so very different from the Afghan landscape. It is amazing what we take for granted and how incredible our Western civilization is despite its warts and squabbles.

The timing of my leave wasn't ideal, but I made the most of it. I had just learned that I would have to be in Norfolk in mid-January, so I would have to return to Afghanistan for one week before doubling back halfway around the globe to Virginia. I had circadian whiplash, but all in a good cause. I was fortunate to arrive home just before Christmas in perfect timing with Broghan and Peter Jr.'s arrivals. Despite being signed into Northwest Airline's unaccompanied child's program, they had been left unceremoniously in Amsterdam's Schiphol Airport after their transatlantic flight from Boston. It took some anxious moments and some phone-calling to track them down and get them corralled and on their connection to Frankfurt. Once that extended nervous moment passed, the holiday really began in earnest. Initially, I simply chilled out and decompressed with the family. But in truth, I was initially somewhat listless. The cumulative stress and tiredness of the day-in and day-out grind of tracking the situation, threats, and bad guys in Afghanistan really caught up with me.

I brought home gifts acquired in the Friday Bazaars that included a large, absolutely unique Baluchi animal-motif carpet to go along with that distinctly imperfect, natural-dyed Golden Ghazni runner I described. I gave each of the three kids their first carpets: all rugged Baluchis with animal designs for the girls and a war rug—made famous in the struggle against the Soviets—for Peter Jr. Stephanie received emeralds from Ahmad Massoud's ruggedly beautiful Panjshir Valley. At the same time, she had framed for me three wonderful period-piece Unicum liqueur posters. We indulged in some good wines and beer. I quickly learned that even a small sip went pleasantly straight to my head after months of alcohol abstinence.

In my half-year away, Alessandra, while still loving her Mermaids and Faeries, has had become enamored with Meryl Streep's *Mama Mia*, which dethroned *Hairspray*. Broghan, having shaken off *Ironman*, had become enthralled with the offbeat, culty *Twilight*. Peter, in turn, was delighting in the iPod he received (so did Broghan) as well as working the flintlock action on a 1777 era French Charleville Musket that I had guiltily acquired for myself to go with my prize Old Guardsman's Bearskin. I said goodbye to our two pugs, Winston and Neville—famous last year for their bomber-jacketed cameo appearance on a European Command Video Teleconference. After four years of affable non-house-broken dysfunction, we re-homed them with two local families who take good care of them.

We then traveled by Ryan Air to Pisa to spend five days at my father's home in Bolgheri, Tuscany. Once again, life and its imperatives here were all so different from Afghanistan. The big news was that my father and my sister Pinki invested in the sole village bar, "Il Bar," that had lost its charm and clientele. The prospect of being the old bar's new owners seemed appropriate: my family has had a presence in Bolgheri since 1975. So, I know where my older kids will be next summer—serving cappuccinos and the like to locals and tourists marching by.

While in Bolgheri, we enjoyed the traditional Christmas that my stepmother Anne loves. On Christmas Eve, set by a lovely crackling fire, we all held hands while she played, and we sang "Silent Night." Then we all sat down and devoured a gigantic turkey. For presents, I gave all the women stunning silk and wool embroidered Afghan jackets hand-made by an older Afghan woman—Zahrya—I know in Kabul. Pinki, who had just returned from months of demanding work on relaunching Zwack liqueur in the USA, gave me a superb bottle of Masseto wine, a super Tuscan now even more coveted than its Sassicaia or Ornellaia cousins. She also organized a riotous party before the New Year that went into the wee hours, culminating in my pouring Barack Palinka not just down gullets but also on people's heads and hair while they danced. While doing so, I carelessly dropped a schlug of it directly into my right eye. My-oh-my did that sting worse than any cheap shampoo! But proud to the end, I gamely shimmied my way to the bathroom to wash out my screaming eyeball!

Several days later, I said goodbye to my family—easier than when I departed for a year last June—and was back on my way to Afghanistan and its utterly alien world.

Parting Thoughts on Part II

February 2009

I'M PUTTING THE FINAL TOUCHES on this edition of the *Kurier* while sitting in a hotel in Dubai. Tomorrow I return to Afghanistan, having completed my ten weeks in Norfolk, Virginia, where I attended a senior level Joint Forces level military seminar and communed and shared lessons learned with numerous extraordinary military professionals and peers. These included the Army Special Forces officer that accompanied Hamid Karzai into Uruzgan, Afghanistan, in October 2001, a former Air force F-22 fighter squadron commander, a Navy destroyer flotilla commodore, a former Army combat aviation brigade commander in Iraq, a former Air Force B2 squadron commander with a direct lineage to Brigadier General Paul Tibbets of Enola Gay fame, a Marine regimental commander at Fallujah, the former 82nd Airborne Chief of Staff in Afghanistan, a former Navy F-18 carrier squadron commander, a former Nuclear submarine commander (both attack and boomer [nuclear missile]) a brilliant cyber-specialist, a superb Army engineer, world-class expeditionary air force logistician and an extraordinarily polished naval captain from Chile—the list goes on and on, full of talented people—all veterans, former commanders and dedicated to service—the very best our great nation has to offer.

To close this edition of the *Kurier*, I just wanted to touch on the situation in Afghanistan in Winter 2009 and rebut just a little bit of the very negative reportage that I've seen and heard. I believe that the proverbial glass is still "half full" over here. While we are certainly not winning at present and are in for a tough, challenging summer, the enemy isn't winning either. Major efforts are underway to break this stalemate and change the insurgency's playing field and overall dynamics while leveraging all possible hard and soft power resources to regain the positive momentum we had with the general population from 2002–2004. I must emphasize polling data revealed that the people, though dissatisfied with the current Karzai government, overwhelmingly do not want to return to the primitive, suffocating Taliban.

While the violence of all types has steadily increased since 2005, I have tried to highlight other less-reported aspects in the *Kurier*. In

2001, under the Taliban yoke, there was almost no one in school, and what studying there was focused overwhelmingly on the Koran. Afghanistan is a very oral society that can be easily swayed by rumor and Taliban propaganda. Radio, not the Internet, is still the primary way to reach the Afghan heartland. Today several million children, including girls and young women, are in schools, despite the efforts of backward-thinking insurgents to shut them down. There was a shocking attack last fall by some young toughs in Kandahar who threw acid in the faces of girls going to school. This heinous act threw most of the nation into revulsion against these primitive-thinking people.

It also highlighted the educational issue that is a central front against Afghanistan's very high illiteracy rate. If schools aren't functioning, it is challenging to educate people to manage businesses beyond subsistence farming or menial labor, let alone persuade them that poppy cultivation is bad.

Medical services, though spotty, are much improved. Unemployment, a significant driver for the insurgency, remains a major problem that we plan to directly address by improved Afghan security forces and the considerable influx of mostly U.S. forces this year that finally will allow us to hold and build within contested districts. This enhanced security will give the vulnerable UN and NGOs a chance to work their magic and create opportunities in creating employment and local economies other than growing and harvesting opium. Finally, we are working hard and increasingly closely with the Pakistanis to manage the borders and create some headroom to deal with their growing Islamist insurgency. If Pakistan were to fail, it could be the crisis of our generation. As I mentioned before, both nations—Afghanistan and Pakistan—are inextricably linked. The two countries and situations must be dealt with in a coordinated, comprehensive manner, as Ambassador Holbrooke is attempting to do. The nascent dialog with fickle, distrustful Iran is also encouraging as a means to reduce overall tension in the region.

To close, suffice to say this is one hell of an intellectually fascinating and complex mission, and I am honored to be deeply involved in the effort at this time of my life and career. It is important and cannot be neglected or ignored. To do so could lead to one or two failed states that in our increasingly transnational and globalized world would destabilize the entire region and shoot negative tendrils across the globe. As we have seen in Somalia, it would reopen the door to malignant furies represented by al-Qaeda-type terrorism and a humanitarian crisis that would boggle the mind and greatly tax our fragile world. Therefore, we are here in Afghanistan, and this is why this mission remains very important and relevant for us all.

A lot of trust in our superb helicopter aviators navigating between unforgiving ridges and peaks across the Hindu Kush.

Picture Section II

The scenic and populated valleys (often exposed to ambush) were the main air and land traffic highways.

Sarobi Reservior, one of the few bodies of water in northeastern Afghanistan.

Our JIOC-A 2008 Christmas card emailed across the world to our distant homes ... with coalition officers and snow-tipped mountains in the distance.

Home on leave, Christmas at home with my dear family in Heidelberg, Germany.

The "graytail" C-17 Globemaster III transport workhorse, on which I took several intertheater flights and saw up close a late-night refueling somewhere over Central Asia.

Holding a Victorian-era British Martini-Henry rifle, possibly captured from some hapless column and then ornately decorated as a trophy in a local tribal village.

At a bazaar next to our base in Kabul, we could find colorful, hand-woven tribal carpets from both sides of the Northwest frontier—after friendly and expected haggling, this piece came home with me.

Author in civilian garb to blend better "outside
the wire" as international civilian traveling within
Afghanistan. The ever multi-purpose "shemagh"
scarf protects against the sun and windblast while also discreetly covering one's flak
vest if need be.

The ubiquitous and always overladen "Jingle
Truck"; this one on the Ring Road headed
north to Salang.

With CSTC-A peer out in the countryside near Bagram with local villagers and security.

The never-ending preemptive search for terrorists and contraband throughout Afghan cities and roads.

Into the stubborn Panjshir Valley where proud Tajik fighters held off the Soviets, and later the Taliban, before 9/11 as part of the "Northern Alliance."

Older Afghan gentlemen in front of the timeless "Blue Mosque" (1481 CE) in Mazar al-Sharif.

Particularly friendly populations in the ethnically intermingled north.

So many limbs were lost to mines, IEDs, and trauma over 32 years of incessant conflict.

A young Afghan boy making the best use of his circumstances.

Near Jalalabad with senior UN representative. Throughout, and often at great personal risk, the United Nations and numerous international and local NGOs worked hard to bring a better and more inclusive life for Afghan people.

With military & civilian peers at the Headquarters of the Combined Security Assistance Command (CSTC-A) Camp Eggers in Kabul. CSTC-A was the U.S.-led multi-national element supporting the building, equipping, and training Afghan military and security forces.

KABUL KURIER PART III

OCTOBER 13TH, 2009

IT HAS BEEN OVER FIVE months since I started this third and final edition of *The Afghanistan Kabul Kurier*. Much has happened since I began this missive last May—developments that have kept me in both professional and personal flux and delayed this recounting of my time in Afghanistan. This will allow me to write things with a bit of hindsight.

Currently, the Afghan endeavor is very challenged, with President Obama and his cabinet agonizing over the troop levels and duration of our commitment in Afghanistan. This conflict is already defining his presidency. Much has happened since I departed Afghanistan on July 3, 2009—the end of my formal deployment.

But to start, I want to go back to spring 2009, which is when I began this final chapter.

May 1, 2009: Early Friday morning is a period of rest for Islam and for us in Kabul. This stretch of a few hours of relative quiet is a coveted contrast to our typical grueling week of long days and little peace. Only an immediate challenge or crisis can prevent us from recharging for a few hours on Friday morning.

It is rapidly warming up across Afghanistan, although the mountains that surround Kabul still have their white tips. The rainy season appears to be over. The water tables are high again, much needed after a very dry 2008. The brown green Kabul River, a dried-out dumping ground and sewer most of last year, is flowing through the city, albeit with a sluggish current.

This will be the final and third edition of *The Afghanistan Kabul Kurier*. I anticipate departing in mid-July (*I left on July 3rd*), almost 13 months after arriving here in early June 2008. Still, I have no idea where I am headed or what job I will be taking this summer (*as of this writing, still not sure but looking like European Command in Stuttgart.*) The arrival of May is a significant milestone that psychologically brings me to a cognitive endgame though goodness knows there is still so much to do here.

In January, I had a ten-week hiatus, returning to the USA for a course in advanced Joint Warfighting in Norfolk, Virginia, a historic part of the USA that I knew little of except from history books. It was a pleasure and an honor to commune with peers and senior mentors while discussing in depth our military craft, experiences, lessons learned, and the condition of the world. You would be surprised, I think, by how much time we spent addressing the essential civilian and military relationship and how important it is that they are synchronized in counterinsurgency warfare. We cannot succeed in these complex "savage wars of peace," to quote Max Boot, unless we acknowledge, accept, and leverage the critical "soft power" (a concept popularized by Harvard University's Joseph Nye) aspects of these conflicts. Also, the higher we move up in rank and position, the more interaction and coordination we have with our non-uniformed counterparts.

On the way back to the Afghan "front," I had an unintended two days in Dubai. After a pleasant United flight out of Dulles Airport outside of Washington, DC, I found myself stranded in this Gulf equivalent of Las Vegas as my Kam Air flight connection to Kabul had already departed due to an unannounced schedule change, a common occurrence with secondary airlines that fly into a theater of war. Lesson relearned. I had always heard that Dubai—one of seven absolute monarchies comprising the United Arab Emirates—is made up of older Dubai and the sleeker glitzy Dubai Marina. The Marina was a major "holiday" spot for many well-to-do and international glitterati, including well-off Muslims from elsewhere. On a more sobering note, it is one of the key transit points for terrorist funds and a playground for the most corrupt characters from many Muslim lands, including Afghanistan.

So, after taxiing around to find an inexpensive hotel, I set off to explore this Gulf Arab megalopolis, claimed from the inhospitable and scorching hot sands of the Arabian Peninsula. With Juan from the Philippines as my guide, I spent an entire day driving in his well-maintained Toyota around Dubai's perfect roadways through urban canyons flanked by the largest assemblage of ultra-modern skyscraper architecture I have ever seen. Here in Dubai, I was a tourist motoring about to observe that which was the ultimate in the new and modern in most places I visit; I'm digging around in antiquity.

In a nouveau riche kind of way, almost everything about Dubai was ostentatious and reeked of showy wealth. Part of the United Arab Emirates (UAE), Dubai benefits enormously from the sixth-largest oil reserves in the world. With these vast monies, they built the tallest buildings, ritziest hotels, and designer shops. Dubai also employs about two million quasi-serfs that man the service industry—mostly Filipinos and Indians—who do the jobs that the approximately one million Dubai Gulf Arab locals wouldn't touch.

I gazed for some time at the ongoing construction of the slender Burj Dubai tower, which looks like a giant terrestrial needle straining upward to prick the bright blue heavens that wash the area with year-round sunlight. (When finished, the Burj Dubai will stretch to 160 stories and will be the tallest building in the world (check out this link describing this unique edifice: https://en.wikipedia.org/wiki/Burj_Khalifa)

I then visited the gated-off and exclusive "7 Star" Burj Al Arab Hotel, a $650 million playground to those rich and famous who crave both exclusivity and publicity. An exact facsimile of the gigantic Atlantis Hotel in the Bahamas loomed over a causeway leading to the turquoise blue Persian Gulf. Late-model SUVs and sedans filled the highways.

Even in the face of so much ostentatious wealth, I couldn't help but notice a serious fly in the ointment: For Rent and For Lease signs festooning many of the large high-rise apartment and office buildings in Dubai. The signs are a reminder that many fortunes in oil and other "bubble" arenas come and go in the blink of an eye.

In my wanderings, I saw the hypocrisy that accompanies the less-than-pious observance of the Islamic faith in the UAE. I've seen many devout Muslims in Afghanistan and elsewhere, and I know

147

one when I see one, and there are plenty in Dubai who do not meet the criteria. While one cannot drink openly in Dubai restaurants, one can readily find drinks in hotel bars. In one locale, I saw several perfectly manicured and coiffed locals in blindingly white kanduras sipping scotch, with sleek, scantily clad young Filipino lassies in close attendance. I witnessed the same behavior in Thailand years ago as well. Some things never change except location.

In Afghanistan, we pay attention to corruption because it directly influences the counterinsurgency and retards the progress of credible governance. Even before I left Afghanistan, fighting corruption had evolved in my mind into the key "front" for succeeding here. So now, when I hear of an Afghan governmental or security official taking a holiday in Dubai or having a home there, I automatically assume that this is a guy who is likely quite corrupt and does not have the best interests of Afghanistan in mind.

Another interesting point about Dubai is that no terrorists of any ilk attack it. I believe the reason is not because of Dubai's efficient security service, which it has, but also because it is the Switzerland of the Middle East. All types of illicit money flow through there, including funding for transnational terror and criminal groups.

So, to me, in terms of Islam, Dubai represents the polar opposite of the extremist Sunni Wahhabis branch. A silver lining of this Islamic "Sodom and Gomorrah" is that it demonstrates that the extremely conservative Islam one finds in the Arabian Peninsula can indeed adapt. In tiny but influential Dubai, such a "reformation" has occurred, including in the area of basic women's rights. For instance, they can drive cars in the UAE, whereas in Saudi Arabia, it is a punishable offense.

Dubai's existence, along with the other Emirates, represents a major contradiction and schism in Islam. While anathema to the Wahhabis and, frankly, many moderate Muslims, the UAE does represent the possibility that a conservative religion can evolve into a more moderate practice. Perhaps there is hope for some form of reformation in the future within the harder, more conservative, and backward Muslim nation-states such as Pakistan. That said, they're still decades away from the more practical, evolved sort-of-secular Sunni Islam of Turkey or locally influenced Indonesia and Malaysia.

Return to ISAF

After spending ten immersed weeks in Norfolk, Virginia, it felt strange to return to my little room on the ISAF compound in late March 2009. Much was the same, but much had changed too. The northern Kohi Paghman range and the lower hills that hugged Kabul were frosted with blinding white snow when I settled back in. We had entered the rainy season—a godsend for Afghan aquifers and agriculture. After years of drought, the country experienced a bumper wheat crop on a scale not seen for three decades. (Aside: It's a little-known fact that more Afghans typically perish from flooding than from drought.)

My humble room was exactly as I had left it except that a fine patina of dust had settled on everything, everywhere. My blackout curtain, fastened with laundry clips, was folded into a triangle to let in the hazy yellowish light. My unwashed Unicum coffee mug awaited cleaning, followed by a celebratory cup of Kava instant coffee heated with water from a big electric kettle. (I once blew out our building's power grid on a particularly hot day when I fired up that kettle.) I switched to tea for the rest of my stay, so the kettle still saw plenty of daily use.

I was glad I had made my bed before leaving. We use light duvet-covered quilts, and I had acquired several pillows out of which I made a quasi-fort for my little daughter's stuffed Steiff giraffe and Winnie the Pooh chime. To her eight-year-old delight, the giraffe would always be perched on my shoulder when I Skyped with her at night. I had a supply of clean clothes ready, thanks to the base's very efficient one-day laundry service run by mostly Kosovar Albanians, who would always perk up when I said "Falemenderit" in thanks. We have quite a diverse staff here: our Fire Department is composed mainly of Bosnians, and our perimeter guards are Macedonian.

Much had changed here in the overall ISAF mission and my JIOC-A intelligence organization. More than half of my joint composite team had rotated out in a scant eighty days, and I now have a new one-star boss, the first U.S. intelligence general assigned to Afghanistan. So much change in a relatively short period means I've had to adjust one more time to the constant flow and flux of this cobbled-together mission. On the upside, we're receiving massive attention and increasing resources, thanks to new U.S. President Barack Obama. He has put Afghanistan on the front burner. (It was something to see the congratulations and backslapping from our mostly European allies after Obama won the November election.) Eight years into this conflict, such prioritization is long overdue, and we have much catching up to do.

To the Mouth of the Khyber Pass

GETTING OUT TO SEE THE country and people first-hand is as important to me as ever. In April, I traveled aboard a Canadian Huey helicopter of Vietnam vintage to historic Jalalabad and then to the Torkham Gate, the Afghan entry point into the 33-mile-long Khyber Pass.

There is probably no geographic feature on the planet more steeped in history or drenched in blood than the Khyber Pass. It has been romanticized in stories and images for centuries. Among the films in which the Pass plays a starring role is the classic *King of the Khyber Rifles* (1953); in his role as swashbuckling Captain Alan King, Hollywood heartthrob Errol Flynn took on the nettlesome, devious Pathans.

Blood flowed in real life, too. In January 1842, as the story goes, British surgeon William Brydon of the 44th Regiment of Foot coaxed his exhausted horse to safety at General Bob Sales' garrison at Jalalabad. The rest of his regiment had been annihilated a few days earlier by thousands of bloodthirsty, vengeful Afridi Pashtun tribesmen at nearby Gandamak in a heroic last stand on a small hilltop. (The Brits glorify defeat and disaster so well!)

Brydon was the sole survivor of a column consisting of about 4,500 British and Indian soldiers accompanied by as many as 10,000 English women and children. It boggles the mind that Lord Elphinstone and officers thought they could march brazenly into Afghanistan and simply seize Kabul while bringing their wives, children, and overloaded baggage trains with them.

The doomed group set off from Kabul for Peshawar in the dead of winter. Imagine the horror they felt when they realized that their nemesis, an Afghan prince named Akbar Khan, was not going to honor the "safe passage" deal through the Khyber Pass that they had negotiated with him before leaving Kabul. Instead, they were attacked by Afridi and Shinwari Pathan tribesmen who slaughtered them at will. This ill-fated opening volley of the Russia and British "Great Game" was the precursor of three separate Afghan Wars involving the British.

For a fascinating perspective on the Khyber Pass, read Sir Robert Warburton's *Eighteen Years in the Khyber 1879-1898* (1900)—his account of spending almost two decades of relative peace amidst the quarrelsome tribes in the Khyber Pass area. His description of the Afridi exemplifies the Pashtun warrior ethic. Warburton wrote over a century ago:

> *"The Afridi lad from his earliest childhood is taught by the circumstances of his existence and life to distrust all humankind, and very often his near relations, heirs to his small plot of land by right of inheritance, are his deadliest enemies. Therefore, distrust of all mankind and readiness to strike the first blow for the safety of his own life has become the Afridi's maxims. If you can overcome this mistrust and be kind in words to him, he will repay you by a great devotion, and he will put up with any treatment you like to give him except abuse."*

I mention Warburton and the Afridi because understanding the Pashtun and what drives and motivates them is critical to the success of our mission. (As I've noted earlier, most insurgents are Pashtun.) The Pashtuns traditionally have dominated Afghanistan and its other ethnic groups and have provided the country with most of its kings through the Kandahar-based Durrani line. In many aspects, the Pashtuns' way of life and code of "Pashtunwali" parallels Albania's mountain and valley clans and their "Kanun" in Kosovo. (I was in

Kosovo in 2003 on a year-long deployment, so I've observed the similarities first-hand.)

I think we outsiders have become better at understanding what makes these volatile people tick but applying the lessons we've learned is the hard part, especially in areas where we have little to no presence. This is a key reason that we need more security forces, especially well-trained and reliable Afghans who understand their countrymen and tribes. That would be the ideal scenario, of course. In the interim, we need more international troops in Afghanistan as well, so that we can dwell with and provide security to a population traumatized by over thirty years of conflict and war and who mostly want to have a livelihood and be left alone by everyone.

I've said before—and will say many times again—without security, meaning a constant safe and trusted presence in an area; there can be no safe development and building by the UN and NGOs. Without safe development and security, there is no real chance for positive governance to take root.

Managing the Pashtun challenge is crucial. Keep in mind that the Pashtuns comprise about forty-two percent of the Afghan population and dominate the East, South, and Southwest, together with a few feisty pockets in the North. That's about fourteen million people out of Afghanistan's approximately thirty million population. Probably two to three million of that fourteen million are males of fighting age. Many of them are in remote and hard-to-reach rural villages and valleys. If they are marginally employed or unemployed, they are already living a hard-scrabble life. Add to that the fact that they see first-hand a rapacious and corrupt government presence and influence, not to mention foreign troops whose presence is of no economic benefit to them. No wonder that these young men will pick up a Kalashnikov or plant an IED for just a few dollars. Worse, if a family or close tribal member is killed in activity linked to coalition operations, then the revenge and retribution aspect of Pashtunwali kicks in, and they become willing and vengeful fighters.

To boot, while finding an alternative to poppy growing and harvesting is essential, the recent decision to terminate the poppy eradication program could not have happened soon enough, in my view. Getting rid of poppy fields without providing substitute employment is likely only to result in creating more "local Taliban." I talk a lot about "local Taliban" because the insurgency will become most dangerous and potentially exponential in growth if it grows substantive local legs, meaning that local boys from Pashtun villages need little prompting from Taliban leadership or foreign fighters to fight. Then the insurgency becomes a popular uprising in certain regions and districts against perceived occupiers, which is what happened to the Soviets in the late 1980s and sent them packing. Thankfully, we're not seeing this (yet) in most of today's Afghanistan.

The overwhelming bulk of the population, including the Pashtuns, do not want the Taliban to return. Nor do they like foreign jihadists in their midst. However, they do want a modicum of security and, at most, decentralized credible governance from Kabul so they can live their lives peacefully and predictably. (As we all do, right?) Out of necessity and survival, they will defer to the Taliban and Sharia-based governance structures if there is no other reasonable alternative.

President Karzai has become, in my mind, tone-deaf to all this. He rules, not governs, along the lines of kings and emirs of the past. He dispenses patronage and favors and isn't working to reduce corruption and build a legitimate state, complete with credible rule of law and perceived fairness for all ethnic groups. He is no longer the intelligent, simpatico, and nuanced father of the country that he appeared to be from 2001–2004. Instead, he seems to believe that he alone can run the nation. His defensive posture following the successfully run elections of August 2009 fueled widespread finger-pointing and accusations of vote-fixing and ballot stuffing between Afghans and Afghans, and Afghans and foreigners—the last thing this fragile country needs.

Karzai could have ended the crisis overnight by taking a statesmanlike approach and consenting to a recount. Or, as a good friend suggested to me, he could have invoked a traditional and very democratic Loya Jirga (sort of a large caucus meeting representing all the main tribes and constituencies) to settle the issue. Instead, his attitude undermines our efforts and sows distrust of government in the districts, villages, and valleys. In the end, if his behavior continues unabated and the insurgency spreads, Karzai could find himself isolated, bereft of large chunks of foreign support and resources, because no country, including the U.S., wants to sacrifice its men and women to prop up a government that is perceived by its home population and parliament as illegitimate. Karzai could end up isolated, vulnerable, and ultimately subject to the fate of virtually all of his predecessors.

BACK TO THE KHYBER

LOOKING OUT THE WINDSHIELD OF the Canadian helicopter, I watched vehicles of all shapes and sorts plying the narrow road from Kabul to Jalalabad and on to the Torkham Gate, Afghanistan's entrance to the Khyber and today's border point with Pakistan. Brightly colored "jingle trucks" and old beat-up Japanese sedans crawled along this ancient path. In my mind's eye, I could picture columns of soldiers from every era marching through the Pass. I could also imagine fierce tribesmen with long-range jezails picking off hapless caravan drivers and guards before descending on the booty, armed with razor-sharp kindjals. Today, the spears and knives have been replaced with AK-47s and IEDs. The terrain has remained the same: breathtaking, dangerous, and not for the faint of heart.

The landscape of fertile Nangahar Province below us was startling green, almost an Irish green, a happy reminder of the drought-ending rains of this past spring. (Within a month, most of this green landscape will have reverted to the monotonous beige I often write about.).

From the air, we peered into mud-wall compounds built to protect homesteads from intruders. Surrounding the compound—and sometimes within—were orchards and fields producing high-quality fruits and vegetables—a bounty that helped secure Nangahar's status as one of the wealthiest among the thirty-four provinces within Afghanistan. The harvests were only one source of the province's wealth, however. Another was the powerful, albeit corrupt governor and the revenue from thousands of trucks hauling every imaginable type of licit and illicit cargo through the Khyber Pass.

One of my objectives, when I came to Afghanistan in June 2008, was to travel this storied road and visit the commemorative plaque at the site of the Battle of Gandamak. That said, I reluctantly declined a very tempting offer from a UN member to travel there with him in mufti and unarmed between Kabul and Jalalabad. I might have done it in my 1990s Foreign Area Officer days, but now the risk was higher. I can easily pass myself off as a UN or NGO staffer. Still, even the remote chance of a relatively senior American intelligence officer —i.e., me—being picked up by the Taliban or some other criminal or insurgent group would have been catastrophic to my health(!), not to mention that such an event would have created an absolute PR mess for the command. Maybe in another existence.

THE ROYAL SKELETONS OF SOUTHERN KABUL

ISAF HAS AN INSTALLATION CALLED Camp Julian that rests in Kabul's southern foothills. These heights played a prominent role in the Afghan Civil War of 1992–1996. It was from on high that Gulbuddin Hekmatyar's militia rained hundreds of Chinese-made 107mm and larger rockets on the helpless city, one that teemed with refugees who had recently returned from Pakistan and Iran. In Khaled Hosseini's *A Thousand Splendid Suns,* one of these random rockets from the foothills kills Laila's father. In real life, the barrage of rockets turned southern Kabul into a wasteland, with help from the vicious battles fought by Hekmatyar's Pashtun, Massoud's Tajik, and Muhaqqiq's Hazara militias.

From the encampment, where we were attending a joint ISAF Afghan counter-insurgency course, we could see the shattered husks of both the King's Darul Aman Palace and the Queen's Tajbeg Palace—built during progressive King Amanullah's time on the throne in the 1920s. Sadly, both palaces have seen a great deal of sadness and violence in the years since. On December 27, 1979, Afghan President Hafizullah Amin and his family were wiped out by a Soviet Alpha group assault on the King's Palace. The assault is well covered by Gregory Feifer's recently published book about the Soviet intervention in Afghanistan, *The Great Gamble*. Soviet elite Spetsnaz "Zenit" troops stormed up the broad marble staircase to the upper floor of the Palace and gunned down Amin, who was supposedly taking a last drink from his private bar after being poisoned by a KGB member who had infiltrated household staff.

The Amin assassination marked the start of Russia's decade-long campaign to subdue Afghanistan. The Palace was converted into the main headquarters of the 40th Army during the Soviet occupation. Judging from pictures I have seen, it was rather well-manicured and maintained even during the occupation. While visiting the grounds, I noticed a futuristic-looking structure equipped with a swimming pool (reminded me a bit of the Genesee building in the Rocky Mountain foothills made famous in Woodie Allen's uproarious *Sleeper*). The building had been converted into an officers' club for the Russians. As the story goes, the club was surprise-attacked one night by Mujahideen, who had infiltrated the property from the hills. During the attack, they butchered a number of senior Soviet officers who were dining there.

I was able to get inside the Queen's Palace and look around. Over the years, the palace has been used as a headquarters and meeting point for numerous military organizations, including U.S. Special Forces, after Kabul was liberated in late 2001. Designed by a German engineer, the craftsmanship was evident everywhere, in spite of the broken glass, rubble, and bullet holes. There were also big gouges, suggesting damage incurred by larger caliber weapons and grenades. Inside, metal and any electrical wiring had been stripped away. Signs of soccer games played inside the huge palatial rooms were easy to spot.

The more we looked, the more we realized that the signs of fighting we were seeing were not from the Soviet era but rather from the horrific Civil War that followed the defeat of Russian-installed Afghan politician Mohammad Najibullah in 1992. (Najibullah was in power from 1986 until he was deposed six years later.) Upon our exit, we waved to the young Afghan National Army (ANA) soldiers who very casually manned their checkpoint protecting the husk of the Palace. They genially posed for us in front of the green, red, and black Afghan flag and certainly saw us as no threat.

Eight-tenths of a mile away (as the crow flies) were the even more shattered ruins of the multi-storied Darul Aman "Abode of Peace" Palace. Larger than the Queen's Palace and much grander than the Presidential Palace in the heart of Kabul, the King's Palace was constructed in the 1920s during the reign of the very westward-leaning (he wore tweeds and top hats) King Amanullah Khan.

Peering through rusted barbed wire at the wreckage, we could see that this had been a grand palace indeed—indicative of better Afghan times. It's worth noting that there remains a slight monarchist dream among older Afghans, who remember such things. Today, of course, such thoughts are simply unrealistic. If such a reversion to monarchy had ever been possible, it would have had to happen immediately after the Taliban was defeated (2001), when Afghanistan's future was fueled by hopes and dreams of far better days.

Final Months on the Afghan Watch

As the JIOC Director, I had several focus areas for my final months on mission. I mentioned earlier that we moved our entire operation from the dingy but serviceable basement under the J9 Civil Affairs staff section to a new, large, modern, two-storied, but windowless building. It is a big white structure (that quickly grayed in the grungy Kabul air) and is surrounded by a wall topped with razor wire. I wanted to find some creative artists to paint colorful murals on the walls but ran out of time before being able to do so. I was sure that I would have been told that this would not have looked appropriately military, but I frankly didn't care at that point. The whole camp is depressing to the eye, except for the area around the Yellow HQ building and the always-calming Destille Garden.

In the old basement, I had a little cubbyhole of an office in the back where I worked on my three computer systems. On the walls, I put up some Afghan art and a Victorian period Martini-Henry rifle and Pashtun tribal Jezail to warm up the cold, institutional feel of the pale green walls. As I spent so much time anchored to these systems, I regularly played music on a little DVD player, depending on my mood—everything from Santana instrumentals, Yo-Yo Ma, and Buddha Bar to Lou Reed and the Doors, which I turned up for the whole JIOC when I was in a particularly feisty mood.

We also tried to keep the atmosphere light in the new building's 24/7-hour spaces. One of our most memorable efforts was a three-month-long Triops contest—read Sea Monkeys—in which an enterprising soldier mail-ordered $300 worth of the little devils and kits and then sold them to fellow analysts on the work floor. The winner was the one who grew the largest of the little dancing water creatures. To set the scene for this contest, first imagine a large military intelligence analytical center staffed by dozens of bright young military soldiers, sailors, airmen, and civilian analysts, including Brits, Aussies, and Canadians, with a few salty old-timers (like me) for sage advice, at their terminals deeply involved in combating the insurgency. Then picture little plastic aquariums at almost every workstation, where these tiny Triops would swim, grow, and keep us sane. Anytime one died, it was akin to losing a pet.

But there were also moments of sheer comedy, like the day that one of the tanks was accidentally knocked over during a serious briefing session, sending a small crowd of analysts to their knees to try to save the hapless little sea sprite. In addition to the Triops, we also had plenty of furry companions, at least of the feline variety. Alas, we were under strict orders not to touch or feed the ISAF "camp cats" whose job was to keep rodents at bay. The entire human population of the camp—numbering more than 2,000—deftly mastered the art of leaning over just enough to pet heads or deliver treats without appearing to do so. Cameras naturally would pop out whenever a litter of cute kittens was discovered. And, yes, there was that general who discreetly kept a special gray tabby in his HQ (a metal shipping container!).

Believe me when I say these innocent diversions were as precious as gold. Because we certainly had days when our hearts and spirits were sorely tried. One morning, the walkway to our JIOC was blocked off because a desperately distressed U.S. airman had taken a gun and shot a bullet into his head earlier that morning. Such events were rare but deeply troubling. As leaders, we had to constantly monitor the mood and health of our people because, for some, being weighed down by additional personal stressors such as the breaking up of a marriage or relationship, suicide may feel like the only way out.

The honeymoon period of moving to the new building didn't last long. The JIOC edifice revealed some real warts, including dangerously faulty wiring that quite literally shocked several of my folks. Add to that unreliable air conditioning that left my team sweltering, plus energy spikes that overheated our computers and other equipment. And let's not forget the short-circuit-prone wiring to our large JP8 fuel storage tanks. Less lethal but still annoying were dangerously misaligned concrete stairs and comically crooked urinals.

I was so proud and appreciative of my stoic team because I received no major complaints. However, I know for some it was an absolutely unacceptable work situation by today's standards, even while deployed in a tough environment. These construction and quality control glitches significantly risked affecting our ability to best support the rapidly accelerating mission. They were due primarily to the slipshod and hurried workmanship by poorly supervised Afghan contractors who, at times, were simply not up to the complexity of the building. Rightfully so, to increase and improve Afghan capacity, capability, and employment, we employ them in construction efforts. In this case, however, more experience and better skills should have brought to bear on the construction of a key building in a conflict zone.

COMBATING THE INSURGENCY - SOME RETROSPECTIVE THOUGHTS

TODAY, DEEP INTO NOVEMBER 2009, I am far enough from Afghanistan to write about combating this insurgency with real hindsight. If we are to succeed in creating the right conditions for sustained development and good governance, I believe that we need to continue to aggressively push out of our few fully secure areas to connect "complexes" of population centers and agricultural regions. With firm control, development and governance can grow, and the insurgency will wither. This is classic counterinsurgency, nothing fancy.

The key is doing the fundamentals right, including adequate resources and forces, which must include Afghans increasingly taking the lead. Given the relatively low number of troops ISAF has deployed, we can take and retake villages and towns while retaining the major cities but have too little capacity to connect them—"inkblot" is the in-vogue word—together into a viable local or regional entity.

Let's look at the turbulent South where I see two key complexes: the Pashtun Mecca, which includes spiritually strategic Kandahar and its adjoining towns and villages, and the fertile area around Lashkar Gah within the Helmand Valley.

To me, they are both at best loosely linked "micro-campaigns" of the sort that includes the major city as the hub and the multiple "suburbs" that surround them. For Kandahar, this means that the adjacent districts that encompass the key district of Arghandab (that Sarah Chayes so marvelously brought to life in *Punishment of Virtue*) and thorny Zheri, Panjwai and Maiwand (yes, the same place as the British fiasco) must all be "ink blotted" and secure. As long as the Taliban retain access to these districts and safety from the population, insurgents will always be poised to attack Kandahar directly.

To succeed in these "micro-campaigns" will require many troops—ISAF and Afghan—that simply did not exist in adequate numbers even a few months ago. This shortage greatly challenged the Canadian-led "Task Force Kandahar" that has lost over one hundred soldiers, primarily to IEDs, since 2004 and the shoestring but still effective Dutch-Australian mission in Uruzgan Province to the north. The other "'complex" in the south that needs to be fully secured is the fertile belt of towns and districts surrounding Lashkar Gah. These include Nad Ali, Babaji, Marweh, and Nawa—contested zones you will surely hear about in the months ahead. These towns and districts sit astride the largest concentration of poppy cultivation in the world, a circumstance that prevents this fertile area from producing beneficial cash crops such as wheat, saffron, and pomegranates.

Finding or creating productive and secure employment outside of poppy-growing would go a long way toward dampening the insurgency in the Helmand or any other region in Afghanistan. Once the area is cleared and held, much-needed employment could take hold, poppies would go out, and better governance would grow. The insurgents, in turn, who are presently littering the area with lethal IEDs, would be forced out to the periphery away from these population areas.

Other key complexes include the valleys that comprise the Tagab, Alisay, Uzbin, and Alishang, all nearby Kabul's western side. The Tagab has been a chronic trouble spot. On an awful day in August 2008, the French lost 10 Marines in the Uzbin Valley east of Kabul. Since then, ISAF conducted several operations to clear this valley area, but because of how easily the valleys interconnect, the insurgents would move back and forth within them, avoiding the pressure we were trying to exert to hold the entire area. All the valleys would need to be "controlled" simultaneously, which takes numerous security forces.

The same goes for the Morghab valley complex in Badghis Province, an area that has given the Italians and Spanish so much trouble and bleeds over into the Faryab area where the Norwegians effectively patrol. In the east is the challenging, remote, and mountainous region that includes the Korengal, Pech, and Kunar valley complex that so bedevils mostly U.S. forces due to the extremely xenophobic "wild mountain man" syndrome up in the Kunar and Nuristan Province area. As I've mentioned, the Nuristanis, a distinct fair-haired, fair-eyed ethnic group, have never been conquered by the numerous invaders and occupiers of Afghanistan, including Alexander, the Persians, and British, as well as the Soviets. (Incidentally, on a cultural note, they make marvelous, crafted wooden products that include gorgeously painted and lacquered furniture.)

Back to the South Royal Fusiliers and U.S. Marines

In June, I returned from a whirlwind trip to Afghanistan's South, which most believe will be the crucible of decision and resolution in Afghanistan's long insurgency. To review the topography and demography, the South holds the emotional key to the Pashtun nation, namely the crown city of Kandahar and its granary and primary aquifer. I like to call the Helmand River the Nile of Afghanistan. With its headwaters in rugged Uruzgan, this life-giving water source snakes south past Kajaki and its important dam Musa Qala, and on to the region's linchpin Lashkar Gah. The bulk of the British forces in Afghanistan are fighting a particularly virulent insurgency, the foci of which are micro-campaign areas surrounding Kandahar and Lashkar Gah.

We flew out by Italian C130 to remote Camps Bastion and Leatherneck in the pure desert fastnesses of northwest Helmand

Province. These desolate camps are the anchor and bridge that bind operations between Pashtun-dominated and very dangerous Farah Province and the main coalition effort in Central Helmand. It was the time of the "100 Days Wind," which blew so hard and relentlessly that British and U.S. Marine flags and battle standards stayed completely horizontal; the winds also embedded fine dust and sand into every nook and cranny of our persons, kit, and weapons. The night the winds finally subsided, unable to sleep, I lay outside on a concrete revetment and looked up at the stars and pale moon wondering about the future of this worthy endeavor and life overall. I had a lot on my mind. It was one of the most reflective moments of my entire time in Afghanistan.

At Bastion, we attended a ceremony in honor of three British soldiers from the Royal Fusiliers who had died in recent action near Sangin in Northern Helmand. IEDs had killed two of the men, both of whom were bomb disposal personnel, the singularly most dangerous combat job in the world. The fallen being honored that day included a much-beloved soldier of Fijian descent. Several fallen soldiers' peers, mates, and leaders spoke and reminisced during the poignant ceremony. Wood crosses were laid out in the desert sand, and chaplains of the Church of England said their prayers. At the ceremony's end, several hundred brown and tan desert camouflaged soldiers paid their respects, each wearing their British regimental headgear. The sea of hats included jaunty bonnets and caps in all shapes, colors, and tartan patterns, as well as the distinctive white plumed hats of the Royal Fusiliers, with whom these dead soldiers had served.

At adjacent Camp Leatherneck we entered a can-do beehive of determined activity. Several thousand lean, fit, and focused U.S. Marines of the 2nd Marine Expeditionary Brigade were preparing for forays designed to gain the local population's confidence and defeat the insurgency. Marines in their olive green and brown digital battledress were everywhere, training or maintaining their equipment. When the Marines deploy units of this strength, they invariably bring all the key combat multipliers of tactical combat power, which includes excellent riflemen, artillery, and combat aviation, including Cobra helicopters and the vertical takeoff and landing Harrier jump jet that proved so effective over two decades ago in the Falkland Islands.

Just last year, unsupported Marines and U.S. Army Police Mentoring Teams (PMTs) in this area were savaged by huge pressure plate IEDs. The bulking up of troop strength here now is an extremely aggressive move by the U.S. and ISAF. The intent is to redress the balance in this linchpin region between the South and Southwest as soon as possible. While clearing insurgent infested areas, they should, along with an increase of Afghan military and security forces, allow the coalition to "hold" key population centers such as the Lashkar micro-complex that includes Nad Ali, Babaji, Nawa, and thorny Marjeh, and buttress key areas such as Garmsir and Gereshk. This area is the largest poppy-producing center in the world—as much as fifty percent. Holding it and making it unavailable to Taliban and corrupt officials' coffers is key to this region, especially if crops such as wheat, saffron, and pomegranates are offered as an alternative to farmers. The fact that the bountiful record-setting wheat harvest of 2009 managed to produce wheat prices close to that of the unprocessed poppy is a huge harbinger of what could possibly happen within this region if only we could hold and develop it, along with the UN, NGOs, and most importantly, the Afghan populace.

Last Months in Kabul

My FINAL THREE MONTHS IN Afghanistan, the beginning of April 2009, provided me with a quiet period to explore Kabul more thoroughly. While plenty of violence raged, the spring poppy harvest season took many young men away from the Taliban and into the fields. The slight lull allowed me to do what I think is critical for any analyst: develop a first-hand appreciation and understanding of the people and culture. Doing so is exceedingly difficult in rural Afghanistan, but it's possible to slip away and dip into local culture in the cities.

Just minutes away from our fortressed camp gates, several of my team and I were introduced to a resilient, well-educated, and worldly Kabuli intelligentsia. I shared meals and conversations with learned Afghans and ISAF staff at several dinners in the city's quieter oases, such as the peaceful Sufi Restaurant, where dombura music played in the background. A few soldiers from our hard-working group had the most enchanting few hours of our entire deployment to Afghanistan at a U.S. Embassy-sponsored Afghan music evening in the Agha Khan's NGO garden. It was so calm and peaceful there, sitting in the garden with an appreciative and erudite audience that was in perfect contradiction to the difficult insurgency we were fighting. Two bands, one from Northwest Pakistan, played a wide range of instruments perfectly, which helped me attune even better to this complex region. And this was the week I learned from the Afghans of the marvelously lyrical poet Rumi as well.

Meeting and talking to Afghans in these places over the early summer, I confirmed that Kabul was at least perceived as a much safer place than it was even a year ago. This sadly has changed substantially since I departed and wrote this in July. Since then, rockets hit Kabul several times, and a massive suicide car bomb blew up right outside the ISAF headquarters entrance on August 12, just a week before the elections.

Since then, several more suicide car bombs have detonated in Kabul, one killed six Italian soldiers on the heavily trafficked Airport Road. In October a bloody suicide attack by three gunmen on a UN guesthouse killed ten, including six foreign aid workers, further deepening concerns, especially as it appears to have been deliberately focused on the essential UN "soft power and international aid" prop so necessary for enduring development and building. Such acts remind me of how the 2003 bombing of UN headquarters in Baghdad drove out the UN there. I am glad to see the UN is planning to stick it out in Afghanistan and critical Pakistan. In the latter, there was an attack last month against the UN Food Office in Islamabad, killing five innocents.

Out and About with the Afghans

I ALSO SPENT MORE TIME with the Afghan military (ANA) this past four months. Assisting them in building an independent and competent fighting force is a key and, in many ways, the most important pillar for ISAF. Ultimately, they must lead and take the brunt of the fight, as we've seen happen with the Iraqi Army in Iraq. The Afghan human material is good, brave, tough, and feisty, but still incredibly rough-hewn.

I was invited to participate in a "battle staff ride" where seasoned Afghan generals and colonels spoke of their experiences three decades ago, fighting the Soviets along the key route I described earlier between Kabul and Jalalabad, the route of Lord Elphinstone's doomed winter column in 1842. During their time as Mujahideen fighters, they stalked and hunted Soviet and Afghan Army convoys and outposts along the crucial road. Some also talked about their later roles as junior officers in the communist Afghan Army fighting the very same Mujahideen. I listened intently through interpreters. As Mujahideen fighters from several of the seven semi-allied groups formed in Peshawar, they described how they stalked and hunted Soviet and Afghan Army convoys and outposts along this crucial road. The geography—mountains, gorges, and valleys—does not change, but the cast of characters does. These grizzled former fighters fought the Soviets and each other and, later, a newer generation of Taliban Mujahideen.

I communicated with these veterans in Russian, which seems to be the common denominator language for any Afghan officer over 40 and shows the depth of some of the Soviet and Afghan communist education efforts. Early on in Afghanistan's communist experiment, the KHAD, a secret police force—with NKVD-like zeal—jailed and purged many of their own educated and Western-influenced intelligentsia. The Afghan communists, having cleansed the cities, then attempted to bring the Afghan countryside under control. At that point, resistance and Civil War brought in the Soviet Army. The primary goal was to prop up the beleaguered Afghan government, but—as we know—Russia ended up trying to conquer and occupy the entire country. The only thing all these proud officers had in common, other than their shared commitment to defeating the Taliban and other groups, was their distaste for the Pakistanis, whom they saw as the source of most of Afghanistan's woes.

I also had the privilege of joining the Afghan Deputy Minister of Defense and the French mission in attending a graduation commencement exercise on the historic Bala Hissar for the spring Advance Course class for the fledgling Afghan Intelligence Corps. This course is a U.S.-French effort designed to inject some rigor, process, and technique into a rather loose Afghan military intelligence effort, which relies heavily on human intelligence. The Afghan military intelligence operation has not been good at supporting its leadership or combat units with timely, predictive combat intelligence. The course was designed to help beef up their skills.

There are challenges galore to such a process, first and foremost literacy, then essential military skills such as map-reading and basic processes. In this case, it's important not to try to turn the Afghan Intelligence Corps into a technology-dependent service but instead accentuate what they do best: working with and learning about people. As we handed out diplomas, each graduate proudly goose stepped Soviet-style to receive his diploma and on the dais proclaimed his honor and fealty to the nation. (I did not see any graduating women.) This was an impressive bonding and binding event considering that ethnicities of all types were represented in this group: Pashtun, Tajiks, Uzbeks, Hazaras, and others. Finally, we stood at attention and listened to the Afghan national anthem at the ceremony's end. I enjoyed watching the obvious pride of these graduates attentively, a number of whom were seasoned veterans going back to the Civil War, Taliban, and current counter-insurgency period.

The visit gave me the opportunity to explore the Bala Hissar, a huge hulking stone structure that loomed over Central Kabul and served as the city's former fortress and prison. In this huge, storied complex, Afghan rulers dominated the area for centuries. In 1879 the young English Lieutenant Walter Hamilton fought and died here in an epic battle, supported by his incredibly loyal 80 Sikhs of the Indian Guides Cavalry Regiment.

This defense to the death, romanticized so memorably in M. M. Kaye's *The Far Pavilions*, was yet another example of the continuing epic and bloody saga linking the Afghans to the British for almost two centuries. Wherever one walks on the Bala Hissar, one can see signs of more than one conflict from the past. Torn down in 1879 by an avenging punitive British column, the fortress was subsequently rebuilt and savaged repeatedly in numerous civil wars and conflicts. Surprisingly, it was not affected during the ten-year Soviet occupation but was severely damaged by Afghan factional fighting during the five-year Civil war after that.

Wrecked Soviet-made armor was strewn here and there in the complex, including a gutted self-propelled ZSU-23-4 anti-aircraft vehicle perched on the Bala Hissar's highest point. One wonders if it was destroyed in the Civil War or by U.S. forces when we invaded after 9/11. We could not safely clamber down the hillside on which the Bala Hissar sits for fear of triggering unfound land mines and snarling ourselves in the barbed wire that still lay everywhere.

I developed a good relationship with the senior Afghan Army intelligence general and his team during the year. As I've mentioned, it is not unusual for people serving together now to have fought on opposite sides in the past. Some fought for the Soviet-backed communist Najibullah government while others fought for the Mujahideen resistance. Most fought on different sides of the Civil War, with the majority of them supporting Massoud; later, all resisted the Taliban. We must never forget that this counter-insurgency must be Afghan-led, or we will never reach a successful conclusion in the security line of operation.

During my last week on assignment, the Afghan general hosted twenty-five analysts from my team at the Intercontinental Hotel. *(Site of a bloody Taliban attack in 2017).* This modern slab-sided high-rise building was built in 1969 during the Zahir Shah era and was the premier hotel in Kabul until the modern, 5-star Serena was built in 2005 (also the site of a gory attack in early 2008). From days past, one can still find vintage keychains, postcards, and posters showing the "Intercont" as one of the primary tourist and cultural magnets of pre-turmoil Kabul. It housed Soviet officers during their occupation and served as press HQ during the Taliban oppression. It's somewhat amazing that the hotel survived the orgy of shooting and shelling around Kabul during thirty years of conflict, probably due to its location on the outskirts of town. It remains a terrorist target; it regularly comes up in contemporary threat reporting, which we took very seriously. We all were aware of the horrific Serena attack in April 2008 *(and savagely attacked again in 2014)* and continuing attacks against the premier, international-focused hotels, which occurred recently in Mumbai and Peshawar.

It was great to see my intelligence soldiers, sailors, airmen, Marines, and civilians enjoy an evening in Kabul outside our ISAF cantonment. Many of our incredible, bright, and inquisitive personnel from the U.S., UK, Australia, and Canada had never seen the city at night. It was good for them to experience for themselves the bustling street activity, brightly lit streetscape, and a palpable sense of urban security. When they write their threat assessments, almost all of it is based on other people's reporting.

We passed through numerous checkpoints manned by gray uniformed Afghan Police, plain-clothed or camouflaged NDS, and private security companies. Redundancy filters out the less sophisticated enemy. It makes access to our vital areas more difficult and particularly chancy for troublemakers, though inevitably "leakers" get through occasionally, as hard as we try to reduce and mitigate the deadliest bombers. The insider threat— namely insurgents who can infiltrate into the ANSF and attack us from within our ranks— remains our most deadly threat, especially in the cities where we are so intermingled. There will be more bad occurrences in Kabul; this is inevitable, but I would like to remind some folks that for many of us, "the worst day in Kabul was better than the best day in Baghdad."

Dealing with suicide bombers looking to martyr their bodies for Allah and Paradise requires a tough mindset. Perhaps it's similar to what was required of our parents and grandparents when confronted with the suicidal Kamikaze in the Pacific during World War II.

The scene around the hotel pool was particularly interesting. While we listened to classic Afghan strings and horn, we watched a well-heeled Afghan group—including unveiled women—enjoying barbequed lamb and rice pilaf. (Admittedly, some of us were gastro-intestinally challenged the day after.)

Our host, a Tajik Afghan general, invited me to take a day's driving trip up to the Panjshir Valley—his home district. I really wanted to accept his offer. To visit the area with a man who was from Panjshir would have been an amazing experience, but I was strongly advised not to go due to two recent IED attacks around nearby Bagram Airfield that killed two groups of Americans. One incident involved the Panjshir PRT Commander; and more close to home the other involved a young, bright, and vivacious Air Force intelligence lieutenant—a new Air Force Academy graduate who had only recently been become engaged. Her death really put a pall on our tight-knit intelligence community.

While we generally trust the Afghan security services and their overall capability continues to improve, the "insider threat" is always a possibility. All it would take is a tip or phone call about our route and time to a bomb-enabled insurgent ring for us to be targeted while traveling through some remote place.

Unexpected Leadership Transition

I SUPPOSE I SHOULD BRIEFLY comment about the controversial replacement of General David McKiernan by General Stan McChrystal as ISAF Commander in May 2009. Frankly, it came as a major shock for those of us serving in Kabul, where we thought the campaign, though faced with many challenges, had been methodically grinding along in a deliberate "glass half full" kind of way. Insurgencies are not overcome quickly. They require a patient, multi-layered approach addressing root causes that affect and influence the populace. Progress was being made on multiple fronts: prepping for the upcoming elections, building the Afghan military, better relations and cooperation with the Pakistani military and other important institutions, some military successes against high-value individuals, and closer cooperation with NATO allies and Partners.

Almost everyone I spoke with—U.S., Allied, or Afghan—did

not see this replacement coming. Usually, when a commander is not succeeding, staff generally senses it. No one with whom I spoke was aware that General McKiernan was vulnerable. When I arrived in June last year, ISAF relations with the Pakistani military were at a low ebb; Kabul had suffered several high-profile attacks; force levels—ISAF, OEF, and Afghan—were inadequate to hold and build. But we thought that some positive progress had been made in addressing these major challenges.

From my perspective, both generals are proven and superior commanders who were clearly at the top of their profession. It was the manner of General McKiernan's replacement—in a public press conference seen by the world—that stupefied us. Most enlightening was the reaction by many Allied and Afghan officers, almost all of whom shared our surprise and disappointment at what had transpired.

That said, I was present for the arrival of General McChrystal and his new staff *(that included Major General Michael Flynn as the new ISAF J2)*. They certainly brought real creativity and vigor with them. I hope it can be sustained over what surely will be a bloody, unpredictable, and most important multi-year effort.

What Do We Do next?

It has now been over four months since I left Afghanistan, and I am writing this closing chapter of the *Kurier*. I must say that if I had finished this tome before the August 20th elections, my tone would have been a tad more optimistic about the mission than it may sound now. In the spring and early summer of 2009, it appeared we had some positive momentum going on multiple fronts. First, and perhaps most importantly, we had a challenging but successful voter registration process that held the promise of credible elections. That would give the Afghan government, whatever its composition, increased legitimacy among its peoples and in its dealings with the international community. The insurgency, though extremely dangerous, had lost some steam and direction with many part-time fighters involved in the poppy harvest, and some important leadership had been shaved away on both sides of the border.

In addition, especially in the south around Lashkar Gah, some bold and quietly successful combined ISAF/ANSF missions were undertaken against the Taliban in some of its bastions, disrupting and delaying their traditional early summer expansion of attacks and operations.

The Pakistani military and security forces had finally become more aggressive in their operations against their own Taliban, a Frankenstein monster of the country's own creation. Despite uneven growth and training, the Afghan military and security forces continued to improve. Substantial U.S. reinforcements had arrived or were on the way that could finally give the ISAF's security mission more capability to hold and build in key areas. It was necessary for all the important, population-focused development, which is the heart of any successful counter-insurgency. What was not going well were chronic issues such as combating endemic corruption throughout Afghanistan, the cronyism of the Karzai government, and significantly reducing the poppy trade that fueled both corruption and the insurgency. Solving these problems would take more time, more effort, more persistence.

Writing this in November 2009, I'm sorry to see that the situation in Afghanistan has lurched negatively. The security cocoon around Kabul, which had been somewhat successful for about eight months, was repeatedly penetrated by insurgents last summer and this autumn. Multiple rocket attacks and the suicide attack against ISAF headquarters in the heart of Kabul just a week before the August 20, 2009, election were particularly jarring.

Sadly, the presidential election in Afghanistan—for which we had such high hopes—became a world-class strategic mess. So much so that it has crippled the critical momentum needed to give Afghanistan a credible chance to survive as a legitimate government and state. The craven Afghan government's attempts to deny the results of the subsequent investigation of vote gerrymandering rather than taking a higher, more statesmanlike profile has profoundly shaken the confidence and will of many nations and organizations that are working to support the Afghans. News of this terribly negative development could not have failed to penetrate the villages and valleys where the insurgency most resides. It seems that the insurgency is increasingly more local.

DEPARTURE

It's now August 2021, and like most of the world, I'm watching the dramatic events at Kabul's international airport. The scenes of chaos and crowds are surreal compared to the last time I was there—July 3, 2009—boarding a commercial flight for Frankfurt, Germany, at the end of my own stay in Afghanistan. I still have the ticket for my plane ride on Safi Airways, a then-new Afghan airline representing hope and belief in a positive future for Afghanistan.

DURING MY LAST WEEK IN Kabul, I had been able to share meals and offer sincere thanks to many peers, including fabulous coalition members and civilians, and also a number of Afghan military officers who had been tremendously helpful to me. On my final evening, a few of my staff and I enjoyed a modest farewell dinner.

I had already shipped home by APO some of my treasured Afghan "finds." Even so, my suitcase was heavy when I hoisted it out the narrow door of the humble little room that had been my home for 13 months. (No surprise, I had to pay a hefty overweight luggage fee at the airport!)

Members of my team drove me the short distance to the Kabul airport to catch my 1:00 p.m. flight. I had donned civilian clothes and an Afghan scarf for the trip. My ticket listed me simply as "Mr. Peter Zwack"—no mention of military rank. The plane rolled down the runway, rose from the tarmac, and set a western course for Frankfurt. Exhausted and drained, I let myself drift off to sleep as I watched the hazy peaks of the magnificent Hindu-Kush fade from sight. Eight hours later, I was greeted by my beautiful, ever-patient wife and three kids at the Frankfurt am Main Airport. We drove home on perfect roads to Heidelberg in a Honda minivan—about as far from a HUMVEE or armored SUV as you can get. The following day—July 4th—we joined in an uplifting and moving holiday celebration with our neighbors in Patrick Henry Village, our home on the base where we lived – and then the good German beer flowed and flowed. . .

Even when I was back in Heidelberg and onto my next assignment, one image from my departure from Kabul stayed with me. As I stepped into the SUV at ISAF headquarters to head to the airport that morning, the line-up of international flags was once again at half-mast—just as they were when I helicoptered in on June 6, 2008. During much of my stay in Kabul, those colorful signs of international unity and shared mission had been lowered to honor the memory of one or more coalition members who had recently died in the line of duty. Sad as it was to see the flags fluttering yet again at the halfway mark, I'll always hope that what I accomplished during those 13 months in Afghanistan made a difference, however small—perhaps saved a life, gave someone hope, or simply made this world of ours a little bit better, a little bit kinder, a little more understanding.

Machine-gun sighted along one of the numerous passes in eastern Afghanistan.

Picture Section III

Blackhawk landing at remote U.S. forward operating base in rugged and dangerous Eastern Afghanistan.

HUMVEE convoy lined up in support of senior visit in Eastern Afghanistan.

General McKiernan addresses a mixed group of Afghan and U.S. soldiers in a forward operating base near the porous Afghan border with Pakistan. Coalition and Afghan force interoperability and cohesion were a major priority for ISAF Commanders.

Afghan and U.S. soldiers side-by-side in contested, often bloody Eastern Afghanistan.

Close-up of tired and battle-worn Afghan soldiers in R.C. East (the U.S. sector), many of whom are from northern Afghanistan serving far from the home districts, some occupied by the Taliban, where their families are.

Afghan Army sharpshooters probably borrowing from the legacy of Afghan tribesmen lethally hefting their long, accurate jezails against a wide range of invaders and interlopers (including those from next-door valleys) over the past couple of centuries.

208

The destroyed Darul Aman Palace complex southwest of Kabul was built in the 1920s by the progressive King Amanullah Khan. Afghanistan's modern woes began in December 1979 when Soviet commandos stormed the nearby Tajbeg Palace and slayed the non-cooperative Afghan Communist General Secretary; it then became the Soviet HQ during its 10-year intervention. They were rubbled during the ferocious Civil War that ensued after the Soviets departed in 1989. During Ashraf Ghani's recent presidency, it was rebuilt.

The husk of an abandoned Soviet BMP infantry fighting vehicle in the southern hills outside Kabul.

ISAF/CSTC-A members at the Afghan Command and General Staff College. We participated in a verbal "Battle Staff Ride" with seasoned Afghan military officers who had both served with or fought against the Soviets in the 1980s who recounted their hard-earned experiences.

In the Bala Hissar Citadel with the Chief of Afghan Military Intelligence and French-US officers during the 2009 graduation of a class from its newly minted Military Intelligence School.

With great U.S. Army soldiers in the austere southern hills overlooking teeming Kabul.

Thumbs-up in a Blackhawk helicopter somewhere over eastern or southern Afghanistan. On one of many such trips, my prized sunglasses blew off in the windblast, scuttled along the floor and out the open side door into the vast tawny space below. I sometimes wonder if they survived and became the property of one of those sunglass-toting Taliban fighters. .

211

AFTERWORD

"You have the watches, but we have the time."

—Saying attributed to the Taliban

WHILE I WAS DRAFTING THIS Afterword on August 30, 2021, news flashed across the screen that the last U.S. C-17 departed Kabul's airport at 3:29 p.m. East Coast time, bringing to an official close our twenty-year mission there. Major General Chris Donahue, Commander of the 82nd Airborne, and U.S. Ambassador to Afghanistan Ron Wilson were aboard the plane. I suppose the parallel timing of wrapping up this book and wrapping up the mission that inspired it is a bit eerie but fitting.

I wrote the final edition of the *Kabul Kurier* in November 2009, three months after I left Kabul and returned to my family. Although I was disheartened—as so many were—by the aftermath of the

August elections that year, I wasn't ready to give up. As I sat at my temporary home in Heidelberg and reflected on what I thought the future should hold, I wrote the following:

During my year in Kabul, I often fielded questions from non-military friends about what we were doing. "Why should we stay in Afghanistan?" they would ask. "Why don't we just pull out?" which forced me to crystallize my thinking on this thought-provoking question.

The bottom line for me is that we have no other realistic and moral option but to remain in Afghanistan until this brutal insurgency resolves itself. However, the insurgency is just the symptom of what we must help the Afghans to tackle and overcome.

First, I believe for primarily moral and ethical terms; we must do all we can to overturn among the bulk of the population, especially the Pashtuns, the perception of lost hope and opportunity that existed so positively from the fall of the Taliban in late 2001 until the first successful elections in 2004. Until then, the insurgency was in extremis, driven to hiding in Pakistan and but a faint shadow of what it is today. Old Afghan hands speak of the euphoria that existed among the bulk of the population after the fall of the Taliban, only to be replaced by keen disappointment and alienation when bad governance, substandard employment, and little material support came their way. If the Taliban were to take control again, I fear a major bloodletting against the moderate and educated Afghans, especially in Kabul, the East, and South.

Here I am, twelve years later, on the eve of the twentieth anniversary of 9/11, rereading my words, watching in real-time the chaotic final physical phase of our long and fraught engagement in Afghanistan. From an emotional standpoint, the fast collapse of the Afghan government and the international mission was tough to witness. From an analytical viewpoint, however, I was not surprised. After twenty years, it was indeed time to depart Afghanistan. (More on this point in a bit.) What was tragically out of sync was the way the withdrawal unfolded. The public announcements, timeline, preparation, coordination, and sheer bureaucracy of pulling out were at odds with the grim reality of what was happening in the provinces. In the countryside, already shaky morale and cohesion among Afghan security forces shredded at a quick clip—a development which motivated the Taliban likewise to pick up pace. As the Afghan security force melted away, the emboldened Taliban surged toward

215

Kabul with a speed and ferocity that forestalled any real defense of the capitol or measured international withdrawal. In the end, it was not about superior equipment or systems, but rather about morale, momentum, and the will to fight. All these psychological boosters the Taliban gained in cascading abundance were magnified as demoralized Afghan security forces simply melted away. This allowed the Taliban, mostly on their fast-moving motorcycles and pick-up trucks, to surge towards Kabul with a ferocious velocity nobody imagined, forestalling any real defense of the capital and measured international withdrawal.

As I reread my earlier words about the likely fate of Afghanistan under Taliban rule, I'm pondering the same painful question I posed to myself in 2009: where do we go from here?

I'm no wiser than anyone else, so I won't pretend to have all—or even some—of the answers. But I do have a few thoughts that I think are worth "putting out there" for consideration. I am most struck by how many themes and threads I saw in 2008 and 2009 became even more starkly relevant by 2021 and are likely to remain so for decades to come. Among them are issues that have long been part of the Afghan way of life: a deeply traditional patriarchal society that squanders the talents of half of the country's population; a lucrative opium trade that stymies development of a modern economy; widespread corruption that undermines faith in just governance; regional ambitions and jockeying among Pakistan, Russia, Iran, China, and others; rugged mountain and valley geography that has shaped the psychology of Afghans for millennia.

Those factors form at least part of the backdrop for the collapse of Ashraf Ghani's government in August 2021. I think there were hints all along that the central government was too fragile, with little legitimacy left to withstand serious challenge. Still, the international coalition was (understandably) so tired of so little progress on so many fronts that we were perhaps in denial about how quickly things would fall apart once the decision to withdraw was announced.

This brings me to a key thought about why our efforts didn't result in a visible and conclusive "success" even after two decades of fighting the insurgency. As I watched our troops depart Kabul, I was reminded of the oft-quoted saying credited to the Taliban: "You have the watches, but we have the time." Meaning, in a nutshell, that our Western impulse to believe that things should change quickly (with enough effort) is completely at odds with how time really works in places like Afghanistan. As I noted in my Introduction, tradition-bound Afghans—which very much includes the Taliban and other insurgent-terrorist movements——measure time in generations and centuries, not years. We simply underestimated the staying power and resilience of the Taliban. Our relatively quick routing of the terrorists from Afghanistan in the wake of 9/11 did not prepare us for a long fight with a scrappy and tenacious local enemy that was able to regroup and outwait the most modern military in the world.

As the Soviets learned to their chagrin in the 1980s, the resistance of Afghans to foreign intrusion is almost Darwinian——a test of the survival of the fittest. While many Taliban were felled by our superior weaponry, bombing, and drone strikes from 2001 to 2021, those who survived became truly expert fighters on their own ground. These seasoned fighters were in for the long haul, giving them an advantage over the constantly rotating troops and leadership of coalition members. (My staff in the Kabul intel center changed so regularly that the task of getting new people plugged in and up to speed was a never-ending challenge.) A grizzled Afghan army veteran of the Soviet occupation period in the 1980s told me that new Russian troops often fell victim to the same ambush sites and traps over and over again. Constant turnover at the troop level meant every fresh force learned the same painful lessons as its predecessor.

Our experience was similar. Over the course of twenty years, our troops cycled in and out, on rotations of six to twelve months. Much like the Soviets, we encountered the same dangerous spots— roads, bridges, culverts—and the same ambush sites. Had we had a force of coalition long-timers in place, well-knitted with growing Afghan security forces, UN-NGOs, and credible governance, the accumulation of informal local knowledge might have improved the situation and reduced our casualties. But the revolving door of troop rotation made the transmission of field experience almost impossible. Because most of our forces returned home to their families and moved on with their lives, the sense of having an ongoing shared mission wasn't easy to transmit or sustain. Coalition losses—not to mention civilian casualties—mounted. In the meantime, the battle-hardened Taliban remained in their strongholds— experienced fighters—constantly reinforced by young, under-employed local recruits and adherents replenishing their ranks and learning from their senior leadership. Some of the new Taliban Emirate's declared leadership were among young CIA-enabled Mujahideen fighting the Soviets in the 1980s. Little wonder that they've been able to perfect their techniques.

Another lesson was deeply cultural. Accustomed as we are in the West to strong central government, we (re)discovered that other societies not only function quite differently but really do prefer their way to ours. (Whether or not we think that's a wise choice is another issue.) Afghans (and other cultures in the region) are organized along strong tribal and clan lines to a degree that can be mystifying to outsiders. To our perennial surprise, such kin- or tribe-based societies aren't necessarily interested in exchanging their age-old and familiar arrangements for our more "professional" approach to government. The Afghans see patronage and corruption everywhere at the local level; why build a central government that will almost certainly mean more opportunities for bribes and favoritism?

We saw this bone-deep distrust on full display during the closing days of the U.S. withdrawal. Skeptical (quite rightly) of the Ghani regime and feeling abandoned by their international partners, Afghan security forces—that when well-led and motivated were good fighters—simply melted away in the face of heavy casualties and a determined Taliban push. Their surrender was sped along by the Taliban's dark assurances that if units continued to resist, they would be put to the proverbial sword—-not a tempting fate. If they surrendered, however, they would receive mercy. Little has changed in the way of basic tactics and messaging since the remorseless Mongols swept through Afghanistan eight centuries ago.

Back to the question of what's next. Despite the surprising but still disputed fall of the legendary Panjshir Valley to the Taliban in September 2021, the complex multi-ethnic region in Afghanistan's north (abutting Tajikistan and Uzbekistan) will likely remain a hot spot of defiance and warlords for years to come. (I wrote about Panjshir earlier.) And then there's the country's opium trade which supplies piles of money that fuels the underworld and influences the leadership of regional nations to various degrees.

I believe there are several possible outcomes. First, while victorious against the U.S. coalition, propped-up Afghan government in the short term, the new cashed-strapped Taliban Emirate faces critical governance challenges. As we saw in the suicide bomb attack and last-minute rocket fire at Kabul's airport, the truly warped ISIS-Khorasan is committed to causing trouble for everyone, including the new government. And al-Qaeda is still a presence. What's more, the Taliban is anything but monolithic; ideological factionalism plagues the movement. Add to the mix the age-old tension between and among tribes and ethnicities.

To boot, during the coalition's twenty years in Afghanistan, an entire generation of Afghans has grown up experiencing the freedoms afforded by education, technology, interconnectedness, and diversity. These younger Afghans—including millions of girls and young women—are not likely to give up their worldly dreams anytime soon. If the schoolkids I saw everywhere in the country more than a decade ago are a barometer, it's a safe bet that the aspirations of the rising generation will not fade, even in the face of oppression.

Challenges to the Taliban will also come from outside the country. The region is shaping up for a twentieth-first century reboot of the "Great Game" of two centuries ago. The players then were Britain and Russia. Today, the field is both different and larger. Pakistan, Iran, China, Russia (via its interests in former Soviet Central Asia), as well as India and Turkey, are all jockeying for enhanced position in the region, with Afghanistan, as always, more or less in the middle of it all. The Taliban, inexperienced at real governance, will have to navigate a byzantine puzzle of competing interests and agendas that go far beyond its own pressing domestic concerns. Afghanistan's neighbors are—have traditionally been—and will likely always be opportunistic wolves, even if wrapped in proverbial sheep's clothing. As I've pointed out, old rivalries and suspicions have staying power in this region. And as such, Afghanistan's interests will always be secondary. This is one reason that Kabul, whichever way it evolves, might ultimately see a non-local U.S. "presence" as a useful balancer from afar.

China, for example, covets Afghanistan's rich minerals and resources and will be looking for security and reliability for their new Belt and Road Initiative—a modern iteration of the ancient Silk Road. India, guided by its own security and resource interests, will look dimly on any Chinese-Pakistani partnering—already in the works—and therefore will strive to counterbalance the effect by maintaining links with Afghanistan and Russia. Shiite Iran, in turn, will always maintain its strong, historical, and cultural roots in western Afghanistan while nurturing links with the much-abused Hazaras.

And then there is Russia. As a likely hedge, Moscow reportedly built discreet and troubling ties to the Taliban during the past several years. The first motive, I think, was to curry influence with whomever Moscow believed would be the eventual inheritor of the Afghan lands. The second was classic Russian geopolitics: disrupt the U.S.-led international mission as part of the ongoing global competition between the two superpowers. Long gone is the measured cooperation that the Russia-enabled Northern Distribution Network (NDN) provided between 2008 and 2015.

The NDN allowed U.S. and coalition members to move non-combatant material and personnel from Europe into Central Asia to support the ISAF mission. (One time in 2009, when I was returning to Kabul, I spent 48 hours stranded on Manas Airbase, Kyrgyzstan, one site of this impressive air and land bridge).

No doubt remembering its own recent experience, Moscow likely calculated that the international-backed Afghan government would inevitably fall, unleashing yet again the combined furies of jihadism, crime, drugs, and migration into the greater region. From the Kremlin's perspective, these malign forces would almost certainly flood north from Afghanistan, dangerously threatening Russia's Central Asian interests (and, by extension, Sunni-heavy southern Russia, including the Caucasus region). It's no accident that Russia of late has been reinforcing its presence in the area with military and security exercises including those under the umbrella of its Combined Security Treaty Organization (CSTO).

Russia is right to worry. Transnational Sunni Jihadist groups such as al-Qaeda and the even more lethal and growing ISIS-K could gain strength in Afghanistan if the Taliban splinters. The entire region is nervous about these hard-line terrorists. Russia, China, India, Iran, and even Pakistan will not be immune to infiltration, disruption, and breathtakingly violent attacks by these single-minded movements.

Here's where I can see a case of "strange bedfellows" developing—cautious counter-terror intelligence conduits in the region, including Russia, India, hard-to-pin-down Pakistan, and conceivably even over-the-horizon United States. The Turks also appear to be growing players. (All a modern riff on the ancient saying: "The enemy of my enemy is my friend.") It might seem farfetched right now (although less so after seeing their balancing act during the Kabul Airport crisis), the Taliban leadership in survival mode may be willing to share actionable information about dangerous transnational terrorists in exchange for vital financial and humanitarian support. With Afghanistan's central bank reserves frozen by the United States and others, the Taliban is crippled financially and likely to remain so for the foreseeable future. How and to what degree financial duress, coupled with internal dissent, might compel the Taliban leadership to act, only time will tell.

Images of the chaotic Kabul airport evacuation will dominate the public mind for some time to come. Still, the fact that the painful departure is mostly behind us clears the way to concentrate on growing global security challenges, including an increasingly ambitious, aggressive China, and a dangerously difficult Russia, as well as a Middle East still in upheaval. We must remember that the world has a been through similar wrenching moments, and we always emerge on the other side. Our military presence in Afghanistan is over, but our diplomatic and humanitarian structures are hard at work helping to extract remaining Americans and Afghans who want to leave the country.

While I'm saddened and profoundly disappointed by the disaster that just engulfed Afghanistan and our international mission, I remain proud of my time and service in Afghanistan. It was a privilege to be part of a determined multi-national endeavor to push back against global and regional terror. It's just a shame that our noble intentions led inadvertently and inexorably to almost two decades of earnest but unsuccessful nation-building. I especially appreciate my JIOC-A and ISAF staff colleagues—many of whom I'm still in touch with. Despite our implacable foes, difficult work environment, and the awful things we sometimes witnessed, I will never forget the positive experiences I had with average Afghans. Smiles and even joy often greeted us as we traveled. I would like to believe that many—perhaps even most—of the people we encountered understood the fundamental good-heartedness of our troops, civilian workers, NGOs, and others.

Let us never forget the incredible heroism and strength that our military displayed in the final days of the evacuation. As Marine Corps General Frank McKenzie noted at a press conference announcing the last flight out, we pulled off the largest non-combatant airlift in global history in the face of ISIS-K attacks and extraordinary but unpredictable cooperation by the Taliban. Our troops and diplomatic personnel at Kabul airport hand-screened more than 120,000 evacuees and helped them board flights out. Our fearless Special Forces, along with those of several other coalition nations, helped usher more than 1,000 U.S. citizens, more than 2,000 Afghan SIV (Special Immigrant Visa) holders, and hundreds of foreign nationals to safety. The deep sadness of losing 13 American service members and over 180 Afghans to an ISIS-K suicide attack at the airport, and in its wake unintentionally inflicting civilian casualties due to a tragic targeting mistake, should never diminish our pride in trying to do the right thing, as best we could, under impossible circumstances.

The many thousands of recent evacuees will immediately join friends, relatives, and fellow Afghans as part of its already active diaspora living worldwide. In the past, when nations like Vietnam, Cuba, and Iran collapsed or otherwise failed, we saw new communities spring up around the world where refugees from those places eagerly embraced the opportunity to contribute to their new homelands while maintaining ties to those left behind. I believe that Afghans will prove to be no different. They aspire, they dream, they will roll up their sleeves to work for a better life—a life that would be impossible if they stayed in today's Afghanistan. I hope that my country and the world welcome them and help them on their journeys while not forgetting the millions still in Afghanistan who will never stop dreaming of a better future for their captivating but tortured homeland.

NOTES TO SELF

THINGS I ENJOYED MOST ABOUT AFGHANISTAN

(I WROTE THE SAME IN 2004 AFTER MY YEAR IN KOSOVO)

THE TEAMWORK AND CAMARADERIE OF working an important and multi-national mission. I have always enjoyed and appreciated working in a cooperative multi-national environment where I hope we put our best, enlightened supportive foot forward.

1. Troop visits to all the main Afghan cities (Kabul, Mazar, Kandahar, Heart, and Jalalabad and some of its trouble spots, particularly Lashkar Gah and environs).

2. Afghanistan, its culture, and its people. So, wish I could have done more outside the wire, lucky, however, to have done anything at all.

3. Getting out the Gate into Kabul and environs.

4. The Northern survey trip—4 days by SUV to PRTs and

HQ North via SUV via the Salang Pass, Panjshir Valley, Pole Khumri, Kunduz, Mazar (with a few hours in ancient Balkh).

5. Being able to set forth a position and advocate/defend it at rather high levels

6. Working with the Afghan military and security forces to include regular liaison.

7. Strange deployment humor comes from being together 24/7 and includes activities such as Triops, late-night Fantasy Football, and stress-breaking outings to the on-base bazaar.

8. Getting to Chicken Street and buying an extraordinary 19th-century Jezail.

9. Brief visits to NGOs such as Turquoise Mountain and Aga Khan Foundation. It is so important to remain linked to soft-power endeavors while hunting the bad guys

10. Blessed Friday mornings, on which in sanctuary I wrote the *Kurier* and caught up with correspondence

11. The extraordinary desire by my intelligence chain of support to resource identified personnel and equipment deficiencies even as secondary theater.

12. Meeting extraordinary people from all echelons and walks of life.

SOME THINGS I DISLIKED OR
DID NOT ACCOMPLISH IN AFGHANISTAN

1. During much of my year, the sense that we were a secondary theater is evidenced by the composite, ad hoc nature of my organization. The constant flow and turnover of personnel with various levels of training gave me a feel of plugging the dike with my fingers, especially when asked to present short-fuse, high-quality assessments, and briefing products.

2. Being walled off (I call it akin to the *Truman Show*) from much of the Afghan people and surroundings.

3. The absolute corruption and patronage that pervaded the Afghan side of the governance issues that we as military could not affect and hampers our mission greatly. This includes not being able to bust highly placed officials confirmed in the opium trade.

4. Being an apologist for my nation, sometimes when we went excessively unilateral in mission or intelligence sharing (in my opinion).

5. Old enough to die, old enough to vote, not old or mature

enough to drink a cold beer after whatever duty hour you are finished.

6. The mind-clouding 14–16-hour day or longer First meeting at 7:15 and not walking out of the office until close to midnight, or even later.

7. No church bells—just the muezzin call to prayer (felt same in Kosovo).

8. "Beyond the pale" issues that made me see red and become culturally insensitive, especially when women and young girls were attacked or abused. For example, the burning of girls' schools. (No culture will ever be fully successful when half its potential workforce remains in the name of tradition marginalized and essentially enslaved.)

9. Late-night, short-fuse requirements from Washington before their weekend.

10. The surreal night in headquarters when PFC Bowe Bergdahl went missing in RC East.

11. Being shown after a mission the jagged pockmark in the ballistic glass of my up-armored vehicle's side window where a likely snipers bullet hit while driving dusty, bad roads outside of Kabul.

12. Did not get to Bamian or Jam—two places on my bucket list.

13. A sense that the mission success that I have defined is perilously close to slipping away. I feel the proverbial "glass" is no longer "half full."

PASHTUN POEMS

I'll ask you in the presence of God,

That in order to go to heaven

Why did you orphan my children?

Why did you widow a sick woman?

Why did you kill the son of an old lady?

Why did you kill the only brother of a weak girl?

—Ahmad Fawad Lamay

"The sorrow and grief, these black evenings,

Eyes full of tears and times full of sadness,

These burnt hearts, the killing of youths,

These unfulfilled expectations and Emmet hopes of brides,

With a hatred for war,

I call time and again,

I wait for peace for the grief-stricken Pashtuns."

-Zarlasht Hafeez, a female Pashto poet who has published a collection called *Waiting for Peace*.

About the Author

U.S. BRIGADIER GENERAL PETER B. ZWACK (Ret)

BRIGADIER GENERAL PETER B. ZWACK (Ret) served in tumultuous Afghanistan from 2008–09 as the Director of the Joint Intelligence and Operations Center-Afghanistan (JIOC-A) and was also the senior intelligence officer for U.S. Forces-Afghanistan. Afterward, he served in Moscow as the Senior U.S. Defense Attaché to Russia during the pivotal years of 2012–2014 that included the Russian invasion of Ukraine.

BG Zwack is a U.S. Army veteran, having served over 34 years as a Military Intelligence and Foreign Area Officer in diverse command and staff postings in four combat divisions and locations such as Afghanistan, the Balkans, South Korea, West Germany, and Russia. He became the Chief of Intelligence for U.S. Army Europe and served in the Defense Intelligence Agency (DIA), National

Geospatial-Intelligence Agency (NGA), and Army Cyber Command. He was selected as the Joint Chiefs of Staff "Action Officer of the Year" in 1999 and was inducted into the OCS Hall of fame upon his retirement in 2015. Multi-lingual (Russian, German, Italian, and some French), he is a recipient of the Bronze Star and proudly wore the Ranger tab and Airborne wings.

BG Zwack is currently a Global Fellow at The Kennan Institute within the Woodrow Wilson International Center for Scholars, the premier American center for advanced research on Russia and Eurasia. After his retirement in 2015, he taught at The National Defense University and lectured college, graduate students, and governmental and inter-agency members at a wide range of institutions. Widely published and with a media presence, he also consults for numerous think tanks and businesses in both domestic and international venues.

An avid swimmer and life-time lacrosse goalie, Zwack writes from his home in Newport, Rhode Island, where he lives with his wife Stephanie and three children—Broghan, 2LT Peter Jr. (US Army), and Alessandra, who come and go, three rescue dogs, and a semi-feral cat.

Acknowledgments

I CANNOT OVERSTATE THE LOVING, patient support of my beloved wife Stephanie, and children Broghan, Peter Jr, and Alessandra, who supported and endured my deployments, and overall Army career that took (and moved) us together to numerous domestic locations and overseas to Germany, South Korea, and Russia.

Remembering my extraordinary mother Iris Rogers Argento and father Peter Zwack Sr. who both instilled in me an appreciative sense of the greater world and the drive and curiosity to serve and explore within it.

Many heartfelt thanks to my associate and dear friend of four decades, Terri Beavers, who took the initiative to collate my Afghan writings into a tangible volume several years ago. With great foresight, initiative, and dedication, she helped bring these writings into a publishable book these past weeks of the Afghan crisis.

I am so very appreciative of the superb and seemingly preternatural ability of this book's editor, Kathi Ann Brown, of <u>Milestones Historical Consultants</u>, to understand and anticipate my thinking and intent as she edited the disparate pieces of my account.

A thank you to super-agent <u>Gary M. Krebs</u> for suggesting to "just get it out there and self-publish."

Made in United States
North Haven, CT
08 April 2022

17972762R00159